Collins

11+
Non-Verbal Reasoning

Practice Papers
Book 2

Beatrix Parnaby-Price

Introduction

The 11+ tests

In most cases, the 11+ selection tests are set by GL Assessment (NFER), CEM or the individual school. You should be able to find out which tests your child will be taking on the website of the school they are applying to or from the local authority.

These single subject practice test papers are designed to reflect the style of GL Assessment tests, but provide useful practice and preparation for all 11+ tests and common entrance exams.

The score achieved on these test papers is no guarantee that your child will achieve a score of the same standard on the formal tests. Other factors, such as the standard of responses from all pupils who took the test, will determine their success in the formal examination.

Collins also publishes practice test papers, in partnership with The 11 Plus Tutoring Academy, to support preparation for the CEM tests.

Contents

This book contains:

- four practice papers – Tests A, B, C and D

- a multiple-choice answer sheet for each test

- a complete set of answers, including explanations.

Further multiple-choice answer sheets can be downloaded from our website so that you can reuse these papers: collins.co.uk/11plus

Non-verbal reasoning

Non-verbal reasoning assesses a child's ability to see patterns and relationships independent of language. The questions feature shapes, pictures and patterns and allow children to demonstrate their ability to analyse, deduce and infer from close observation.

Non-verbal reasoning tests provide schools with an indication of a child's potential to work successfully with abstract concepts. The results are good indicators of future learning and success in a number of subject areas.

It is particularly important to provide non-verbal reasoning practice as your child may not have come across this type of question before.

Getting ready for the tests

Spend some time talking with your child before they take the tests, so that they understand the purpose of the practice papers and how doing them will help them to prepare for the actual exam.

Agree with your child a good time to take the practice papers. This should be when they are fresh and alert. You also need to find a good place to work, a place that is comfortable and free from distractions. Being able to see a clock is helpful as they learn how to pace themselves.

Explain how they may find some parts easy and others more challenging, but that they need to have a go at every question. If they 'get stuck' on a question, they should just mark it with an asterisk and carry on. At the end of the paper they may have time to go back and try again.

Multiple-choice tests

For this style of test, the answers are recorded on a separate answer sheet and not in the book. This answer sheet will often be marked by a computer in the actual exam, so it is important that it is used correctly. Answers should be indicated by drawing a clear pencil line through the appropriate box and there should be no other marks. If your child indicates one answer and then wants to change their response, the first mark must be fully rubbed out. Practising with an answer sheet now will reduce the chance of your child getting anxious or confused during the actual test.

The test questions

Each test is made up of five sections, with instructions, an example and some practice questions at the beginning of each section, followed by 12 questions. In the actual exam, each section would be administered and timed separately, with the invigilator reading out the instructions, checking the practice questions and then timing the section. For the purposes of practising, however, the papers can be used in different ways, and three options are set out below.

OPTION 1: Read through the instructions with your child. Get them to complete the practice questions and check the answer key, then allow six minutes for the 12 test questions. If they have not finished in the time, ask them to mark the question they are on and then complete the section. When marking the test, you will be able to see how many questions would have been answered correctly in the time available. Repeat for the other four sections. This option is closest to the real exam.

OPTION 2: Ask your child to read through the instructions and the example at the beginning of the first section themselves. Get them to complete the practice questions and check the answer key, then allow six minutes for the 12 test questions. If they have not finished the section in the time, ask them to mark the question they are on and then complete the section. When marking the test later, you will be able to see how many questions would have been answered correctly in the time available. Repeat this process for the other four sections.

OPTION 3: Simply give the practice paper to your child and get them to read the instructions and work through the paper by themselves without any help or guidance. They should work through the questions with a clock/watch/timer to help them practise working within the allowed time. They will need to be told to ignore the instruction 'Wait until you are told to go on' written in the papers. This option would not provide any opportunity to check answers to the practice questions before working through the paper.

And finally...

Let your child know that tests are just one part of school life and that doing their best is what matters. Plan a fun incentive for after the 11+ tests, such as a day out.

Contents

ACKNOWLEDGEMENTS

The author and publisher are grateful to the copyright holders for permission to use quoted materials and images.

Every effort has been made to trace copyright holders and obtain their permission for the use of copyright material. The author and publisher will gladly receive information enabling them to rectify any error or omission in subsequent editions. All facts are correct at time of going to press.

Published by Collins
An imprint of HarperCollinsPublishers Limited
1 London Bridge Street
London SE1 9GF

HarperCollinsPublishers
Macken House, 39/40 Mayor Street Upper,
Dublin 1, D01 C9W8, Ireland

ISBN 9780008278052

First published 2018
This edition published 2020
Previously published by Letts

10 9 8

© HarperCollinsPublishers Limited 2020

All rights reserved. No part of this publication may be reproduced, stored in a retrieval system, or transmitted, in any form or by any means, electronic, mechanical, photocopying, recording or otherwise, without the prior permission of Collins.

British Library Cataloguing in Publication Data.

A CIP record of this book is available from the British Library.

Commissioning Editors: Michelle I'Anson and Alison James
Author: Beatrix Parnaby-Price
Project Management: Fiona Watson
Cover Design: Kevin Robbins and Sarah Duxbury
Production: Natalia Rebow
Printed by Ashford Colour Press Ltd

MIX
Paper | Supporting
responsible forestry
FSC™ C007454

This book contains FSC™ certified paper and other controlled sources to ensure responsible forest management.

For more information visit: www.harpercollins.co.uk/green

Non-Verbal Reasoning
Multiple-Choice
Practice Test A

Read these instructions carefully.

1. You must not open or turn over this booklet until you are told to do so.

2. The booklet contains a multiple-choice test, in which you have to mark your answer to each question on the separate answer sheet.

3. There are five sections in this test. Each section starts with an explanation of what to do, followed by one or two examples. Explanations of the answers for these are included on the answer sheet. You will then be asked to do some practice questions.

4. You should indicate one answer only for each question by drawing a firm pencil line clearly through the rectangle next to your answer on the answer sheet. Rub out any mistakes as well as you can and put in your new answer.

5. Complete the questions as quickly and carefully as you can. If you find that you cannot do a question, do not waste time on it but go on to the next one.

6. You should do any rough working on a separate sheet of paper.

Section 1

In each of the questions below, there is a sequence of squares with one square left empty. Look at the five squares on the right and find the one that should take the place of the empty square to complete the sequence. Mark it on your answer sheet.

Here is an example to help you.

Example

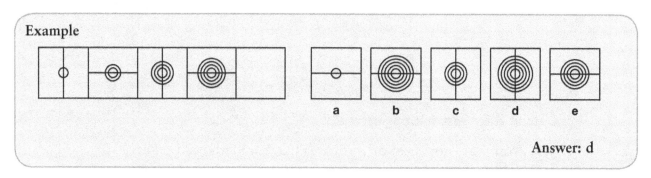

Answer: d

Now try these practice questions.

P1.

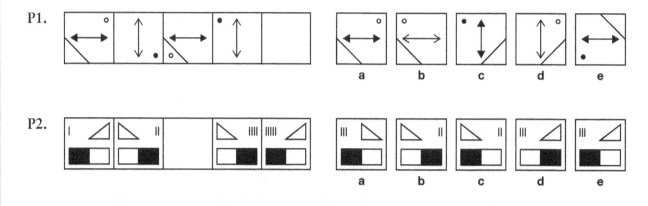

P2.

WAIT UNTIL YOU ARE TOLD TO GO ON

1.

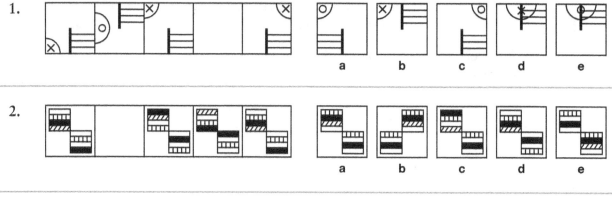

2.

3.

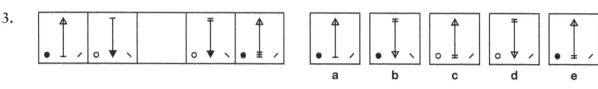

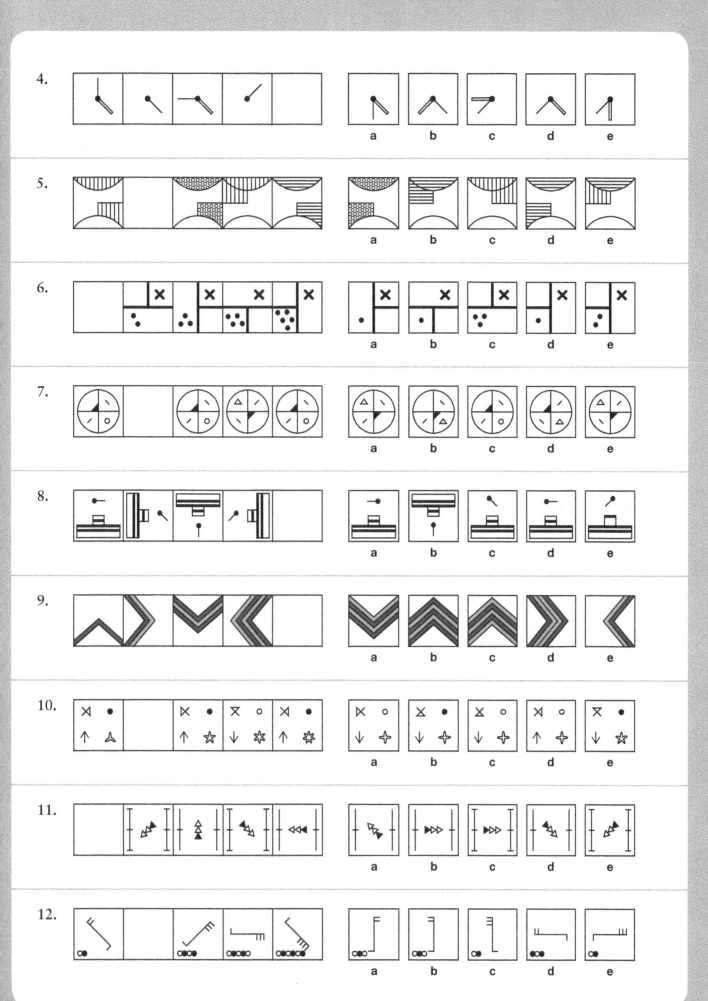

Section 2

In each question below, there are two shapes or patterns on the left which are similar in some way. Decide how they are similar. Find which of the five shapes on the right is most like the two shapes. Mark it on the answer sheet.

Here is an example to help you.

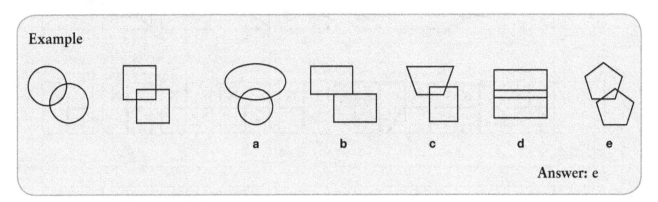

Example

a   b   c   d   e

Answer: e

Now try these practice questions.

P1.

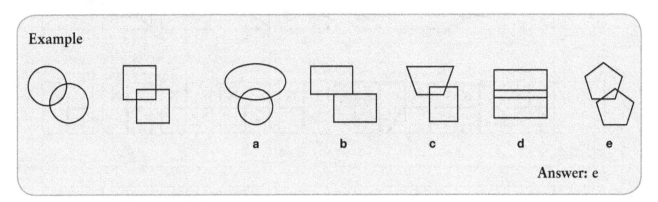

a   b   c   d   e

P2.

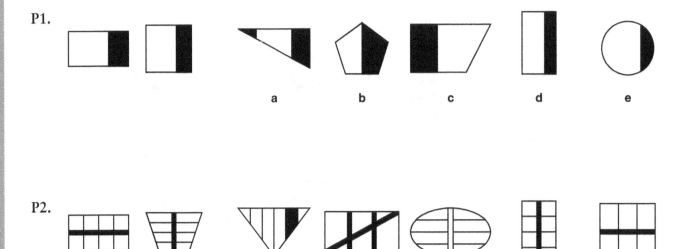

a   b   c   d   e

P3.

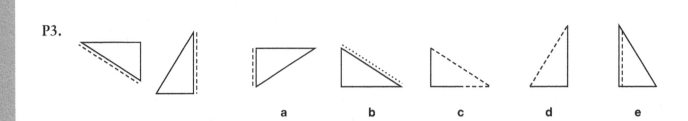

a   b   c   d   e

1.

a   b   c   d   e

2.

a   b   c   d   e

3.

a   b   c   d   e

4.

a   b   c   d   e

5.

a   b   c   d   e

6.

a   b   c   d   e

7.

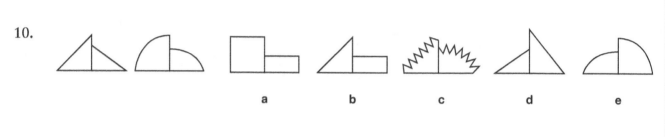

a   b   c   d   e

8.

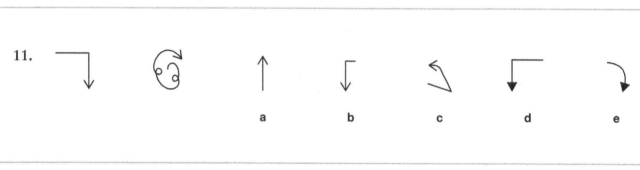

a   b   c   d   e

9.

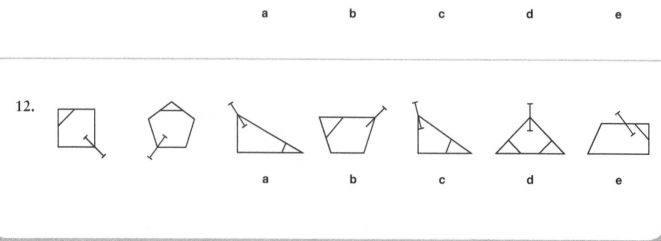

a   b   c   d   e

10.

a   b   c   d   e

11.

a   b   c   d   e

12.

a   b   c   d   e

Section 3

In each of the questions below, there are two shapes on the left with an arrow between them. Look at them carefully and decide how the second shape is related to the first shape. There is then a third shape and another arrow followed by five more shapes. Decide which of the five shapes completes the second pair in the same way as the first pair. Mark it on your answer sheet.

Here is an example to help you.

Example

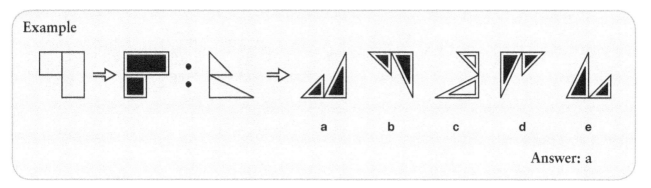

a   b   c   d   e

Answer: a

Now try these practice questions.

P1.

                                       a   b   c   d   e

P2.

                                         a   b   c   d   e

WAIT UNTIL YOU ARE TOLD TO GO ON

1.

                                         a   b   c   d   e

2.

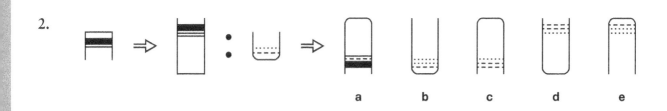

                                         a   b   c   d   e

3.

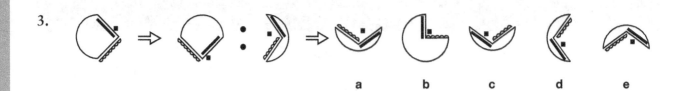

                  a   b   c   d   e

4.

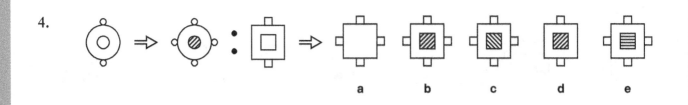

                  a   b   c   d   e

5.

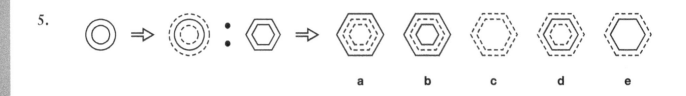

                  a   b   c   d   e

6.

                  a   b   c   d   e

7.

                  a   b   c   d   e

8.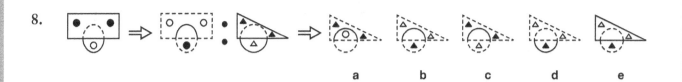

a b c d e

9.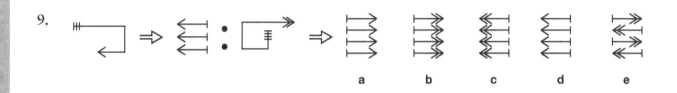

a b c d e

10.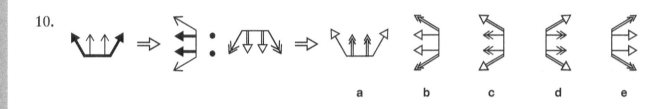

a b c d e

11.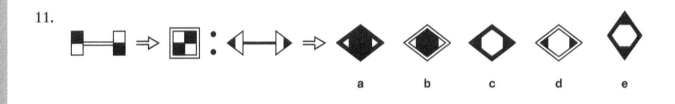

a b c d e

12.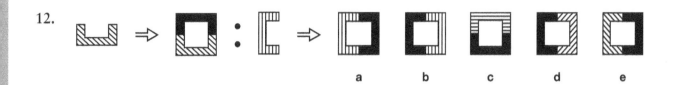

a b c d e

Section 4

In the grids below, one square has been left empty. Look carefully at the five squares to the right and select the square that should complete the grid. Mark it on your answer sheet.

Here is an example to help you.

Example

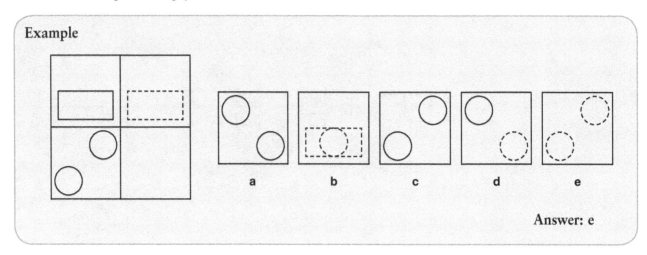

Answer: e

Now try these practice questions.

P1.

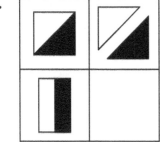   

a   b   c   d   e

P2.

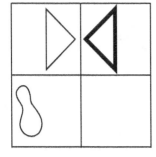    

a   b   c   d   e

P3.

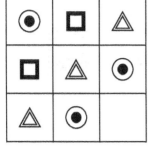

a   b   c   d   e

P4.

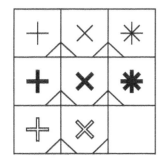

a   b   c   d   e

WAIT UNTIL YOU ARE TOLD TO GO ON

1.

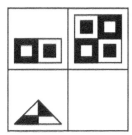

a   b   c   d   e

2.

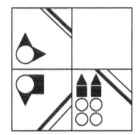

a   b   c   d   e

3.

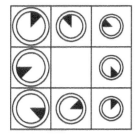

a   b   c   d   e

4.

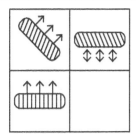

a   b   c   d   e

5.

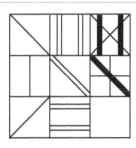

a   b   c   d   e

NOW GO ON TO THE NEXT PAGE

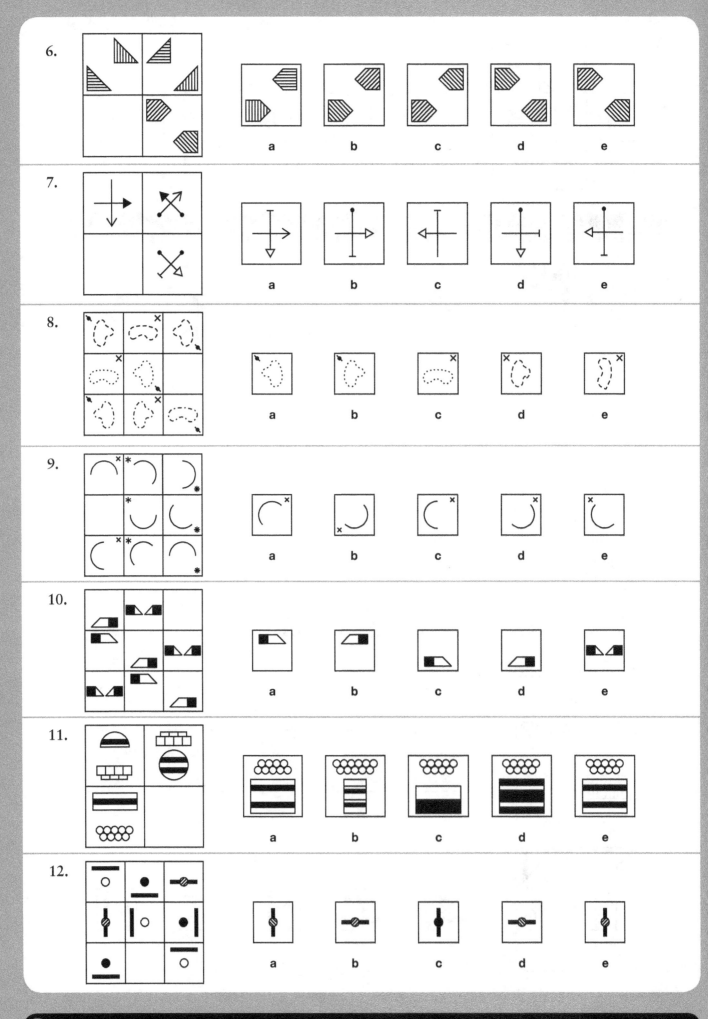

In the questions below, you have to work out a code. You are given some shapes and the codes that go with them. Decide how the codes match the shapes. Then look at the test shape and find its correct code from the five given on the right. Mark it on your answer sheet.

Here are two examples to help you.

Look at Example 1.

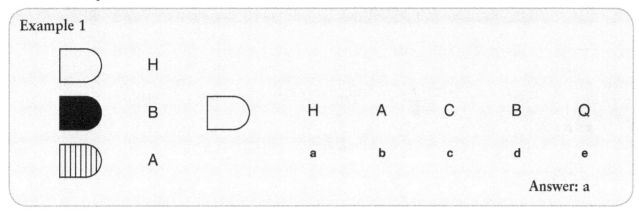

H stands for a white shape, B for a dark shape and A for a striped shape, so the code for the shape must be H.

Now look at Example 2.

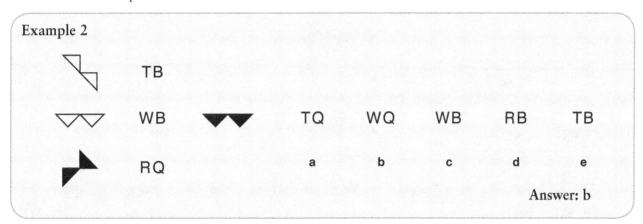

This time the shapes on the left have two letters. Find two shapes that have a letter in common. The first and second shapes both have the letter B as the second letter of the code, so B must be the code for shading. The first letter is different for each shape, so the first letter must be the code for the position of the triangles. The test shape is the same shape as the second shape, with dark shading, so its code is WQ. WQ is option **b**, so **b** is the correct answer.

Now try these practice questions.

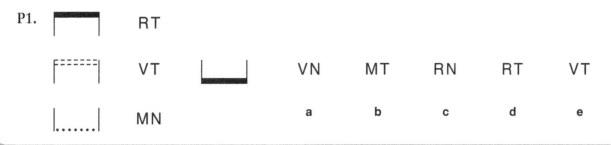

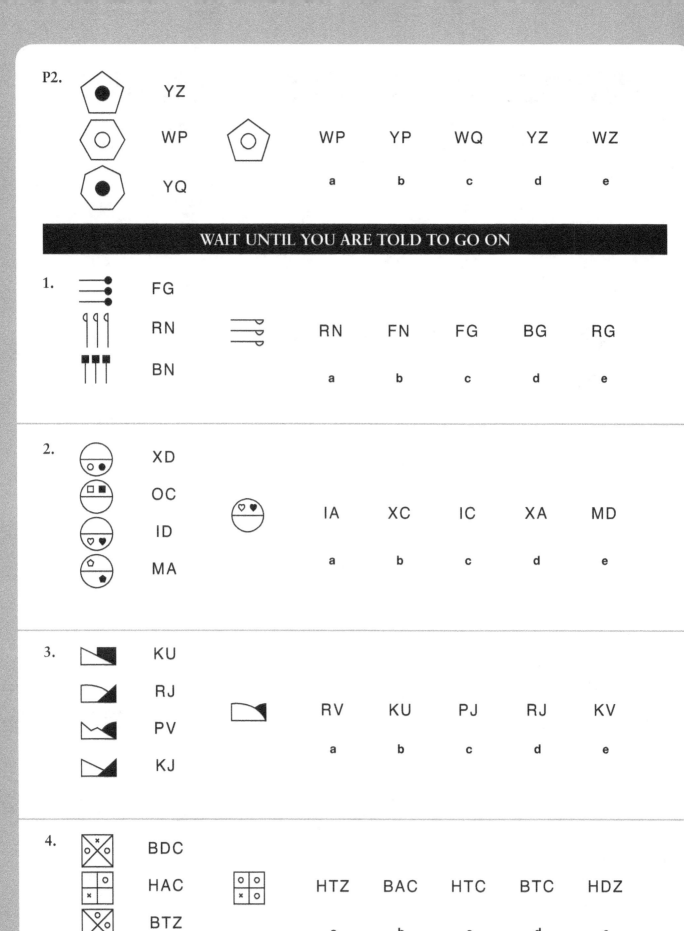

P2.

		WP	YP	WQ	YZ	WZ
		a	b	c	d	e

YZ
WP
YQ

WAIT UNTIL YOU ARE TOLD TO GO ON

1.

FG
RN
BN

RN	FN	FG	BG	RG
a	b	c	d	e

2.

XD
OC
ID
MA

IA	XC	IC	XA	MD
a	b	c	d	e

3.

KU
RJ
PV
KJ

RV	KU	PJ	RJ	KV
a	b	c	d	e

4.

BDC
HAC
BTZ

HTZ	BAC	HTC	BTC	HDZ
a	b	c	d	e

NOW GO ON TO THE NEXT PAGE

5.

YP
XP 
UG 

	YP	XP	UG	YG	UP
	a	b	c	d	e

6.

RAJ
PAG 
OBU 
VBG 

	OAU	VAG	RBC	RBU	RAU
	a	b	c	d	e

7.

DF
SW 
DP 

	SF	DW	DF	SP	DP
	a	b	c	d	e

8.

BAC
BRD 
OFC 
OQD 

	ORC	BAD	OQC	BAC	BFD
	a	b	c	d	e

9.

DBX
REQ 
WZU 
DEU 

	RBX	RZX	WEQ	DBX	DZU
	a	b	c	d	e

NOW GO ON TO THE NEXT PAGE

10.

		LW	SM	SW	SN	LN
⊠•	SW	a	b	c	d	e
⊠▲	LM					
⊠•	SN					

11.

		FLV	KOI	ALI	FOP	COV
↑	KLI	a	b	c	d	e
↓	ALP					
↗	COI					
↖	FOV					

12.

		KXW	MQP	RXP	KQW	MXP
☆	KXP	a	b	c	d	e
☆	RQP					
☆	MXW					

Non-Verbal Reasoning
Multiple-Choice
Practice Test B

Read these instructions carefully.

1. You must not open or turn over this booklet until you are told to do so.

2. The booklet contains a multiple-choice test, in which you have to mark your answer to each question on the separate answer sheet.

3. There are five sections in this test. Each section starts with an explanation of what to do, followed by one or two examples. Explanations of the answers for these are included on the answer sheet. You will then be asked to do some practice questions.

4. You should indicate one answer only for each question by drawing a firm pencil line clearly through the rectangle next to your answer on the answer sheet. Rub out any mistakes as well as you can and put in your new answer.

5. Complete the questions as quickly and carefully as you can. If you find that you cannot do a question, do not waste time on it but go on to the next one.

6. You should do any rough working on a separate sheet of paper.

Section 1

In each of the questions below, there are two shapes on the left with an arrow between them. Look at them carefully and decide how the second shape is related to the first shape. There is then a third shape and another arrow followed by five more shapes. Decide which of the five shapes completes the second pair in the same way as the first pair. Mark it on your answer sheet.

Here is an example to help you.

Example

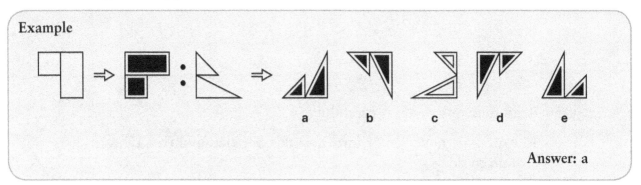

Answer: a

Now try these practice questions.

P1.

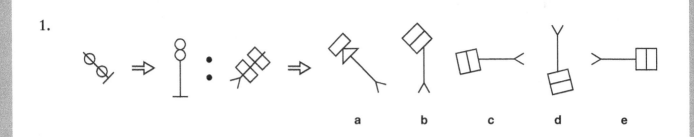

P2.

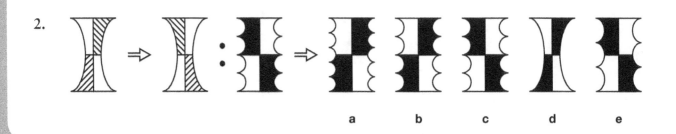

WAIT UNTIL YOU ARE TOLD TO GO ON

1.

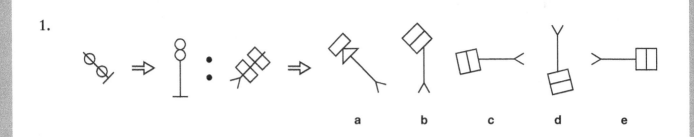

2.

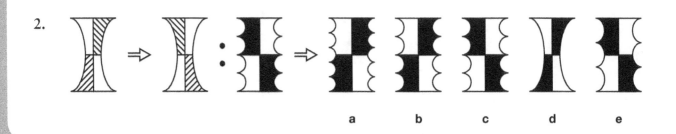

3.

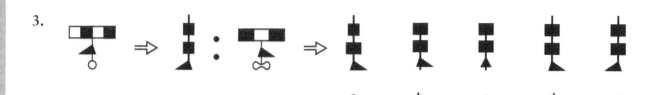

a   b   c   d   e

4.

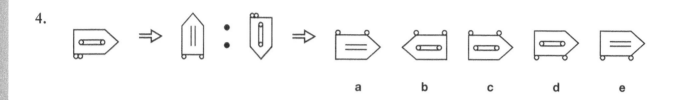

a   b   c   d   e

5.

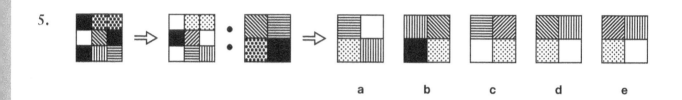

a   b   c   d   e

6.

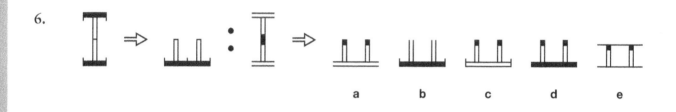

a   b   c   d   e

7.

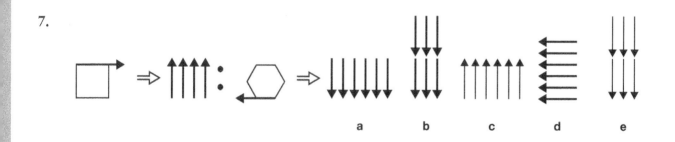

a   b   c   d   e

8.

a   b   c   d   e

9.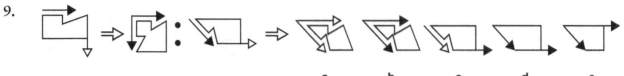

a   b   c   d   e

10.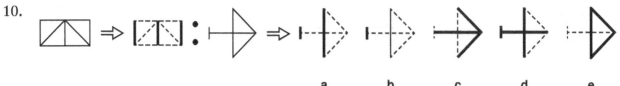

a   b   c   d   e

11.

a   b   c   d   e

12.

a   b   c   d   e

Section 2

In the grids below, one square has been left empty. Look carefully at the five squares to the right and select the square that should complete the grid. Mark it on your answer sheet.

Here is an example to help you.

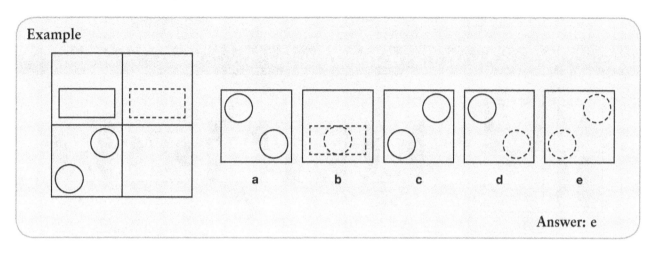

Answer: e

Now try these practice questions.

P1.

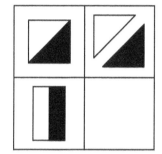
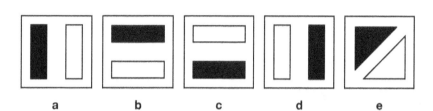

P2.

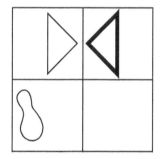
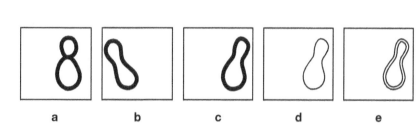

P3.

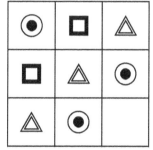
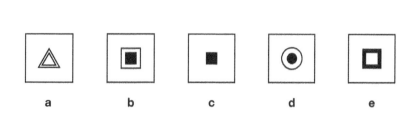

P4.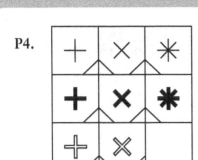

a   b   c   d   e

WAIT UNTIL YOU ARE TOLD TO GO ON

1.

a   b   c   d   e

2.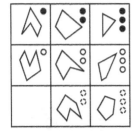

a   b   c   d   e

3.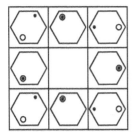

a   b   c   d   e

4.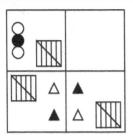

a   b   c   d   e

5.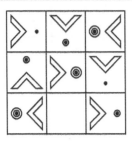

a   b   c   d   e

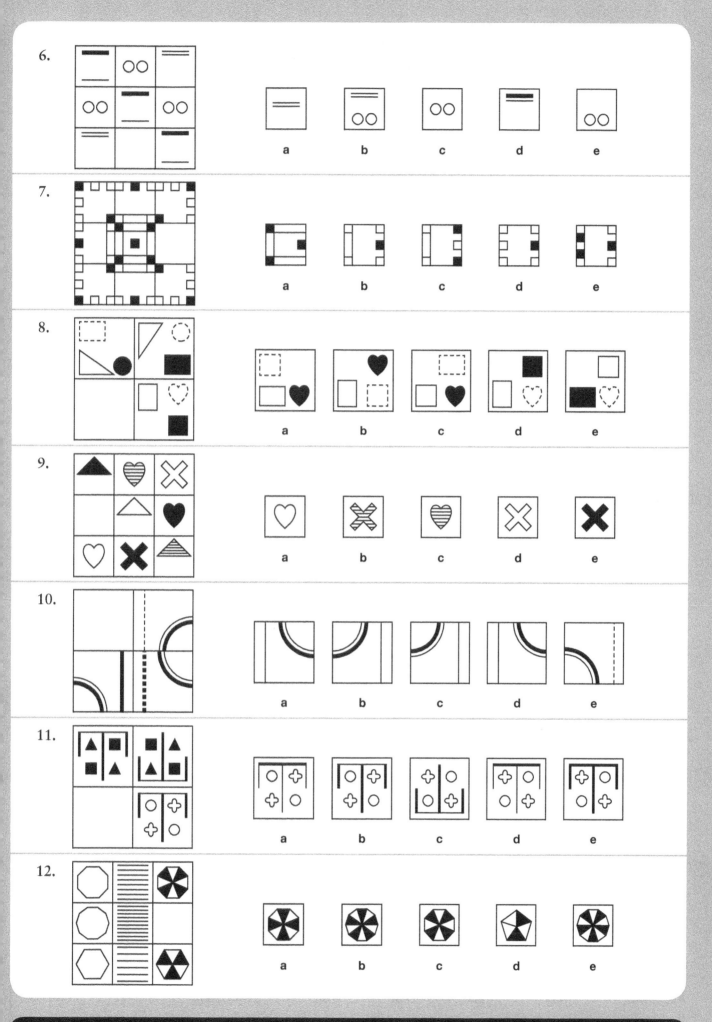

6.

7.

8.

9.

10.

11.

12.

In the questions below, you have to work out a code. You are given some shapes and the codes that go with them. Decide how the codes match the shapes. Then look at the test shape and find its correct code from the five given on the right. Mark it on your answer sheet.

Here are two examples to help you.

Look at Example 1.

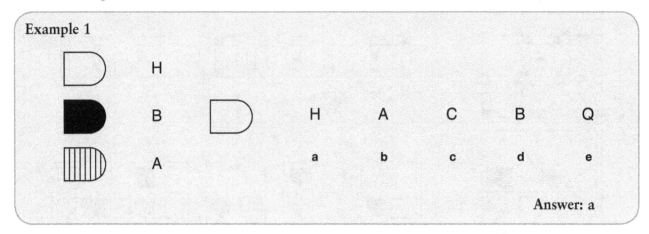

Example 1

			H	A	C	B	Q
			a	b	c	d	e

Answer: a

H stands for a white shape, B for a dark shape and A for a striped shape, so the code for the shape must be H.

Now look at Example 2.

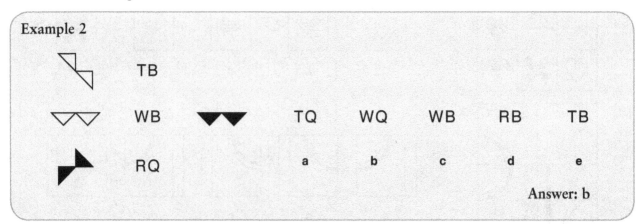

Example 2

			TQ	WQ	WB	RB	TB
			a	b	c	d	e

Answer: b

This time the shapes on the left have two letters. Find two shapes that have a letter in common. The first and second shapes both have the letter B as the second letter of the code, so B must be the code for shading. The first letter is different for each shape, so the first letter must be the code for the position of the triangles. The test shape is the same shape as the second shape, with dark shading, so its code is WQ. WQ is option **b**, so **b** is the correct answer.

Now try these practice questions.

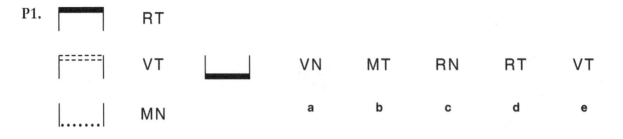

P1.

		VN	MT	RN	RT	VT
		a	b	c	d	e

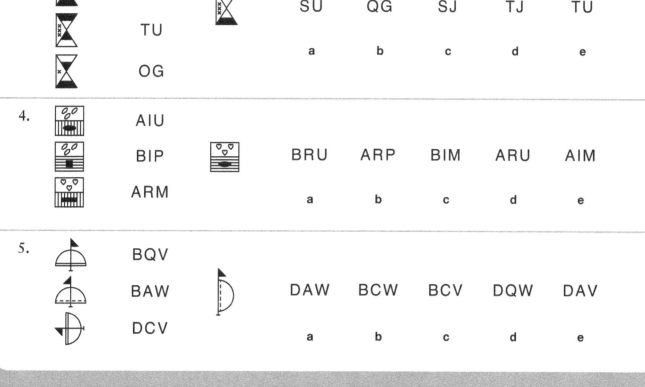

P2.

YZ

WP · · · WP · YP · WQ · YZ · WZ

YQ · · · a · b · c · d · e

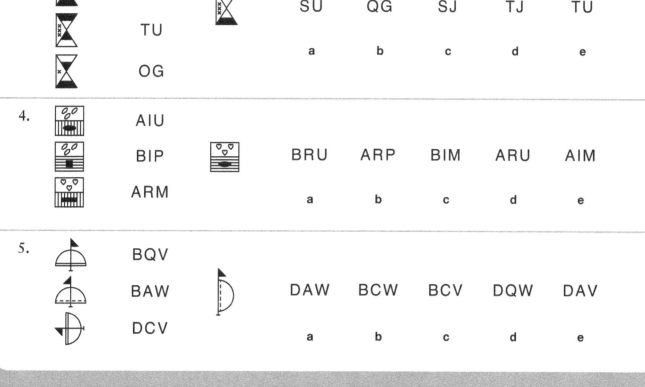

WAIT UNTIL YOU ARE TOLD TO GO ON

1.

VD

PB · · · VA · PD · VB · PA · PB

PA · · · a · b · c · d · e

2.

FR

GM

FV · · · HV · GR · FM · HM · GN

HN · · · a · b · c · d · e

3.

QJ

SG

TU · · · SU · QG · SJ · TJ · TU

OG · · · a · b · c · d · e

4.

AIU

BIP · · · BRU · ARP · BIM · ARU · AIM

ARM · · · a · b · c · d · e

5.

BQV

BAW · · · DAW · BCW · BCV · DQW · DAV

DCV · · · a · b · c · d · e

6.

	LB
	TO
	LS
	TE

	LE	TB	LO	TS	LB
	a	b	c	d	e

7.

	SP
	SX
	WA
	YA

	YA	YP	WX	SP	SX
	a	b	c	d	e

8.

	YO
	PD
	YN

	PD	PO	YD	PN	YN
	a	b	c	d	e

9.

	JQD
	GKD
	GQC
	NRC

	NKD	GRC	NQD	GRD	JKC
	a	b	c	d	e

10.

	FE
	AN
	HN

	HN	FN	AE	AN	HE
	a	b	c	d	e

11.

	VBQ
	RBQ
	VBP
	RWN

	VBN	VWP	RBN	RWQ	RBP
	a	b	c	d	e

12.

	QXH
	QYB
	MTB
	WXH

	WXH	MYB	MXH	WYB	QTH
	a	b	c	d	e

WAIT UNTIL YOU ARE TOLD TO GO ON

Section 4

In each of the questions below, there is a sequence of squares with one square left empty. Look at the five squares on the right and find the one that should take the place of the empty square to complete the sequence. Mark it on your answer sheet.

Here is an example to help you.

Example

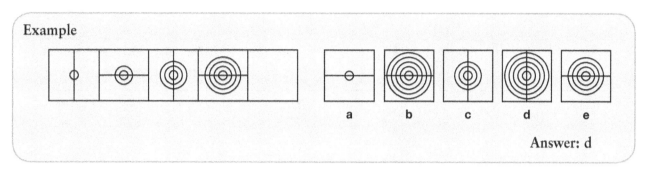

a   b   c   d   e

Answer: d

Now try these practice questions.

P1.

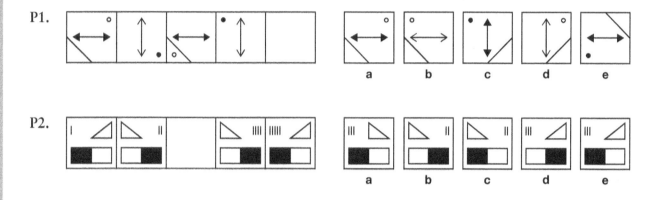

P2.

WAIT UNTIL YOU ARE TOLD TO GO ON

1.

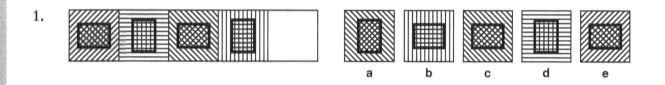

2.

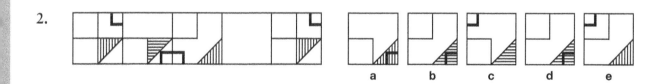

3.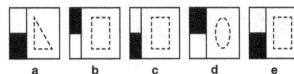

a   b   c   d   e

4.

a   b   c   d   e

5.

a   b   c   d   e

6.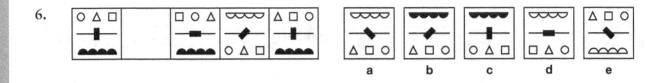

a   b   c   d   e

7.

a   b   c   d   e

8.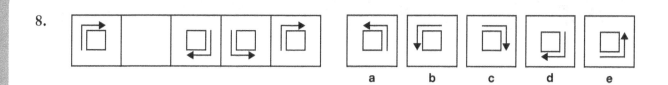

a b c d e

9.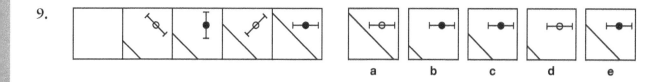

a b c d e

10.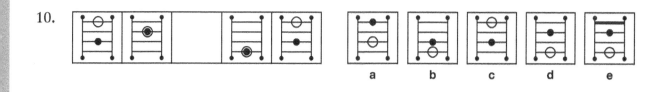

a b c d e

11.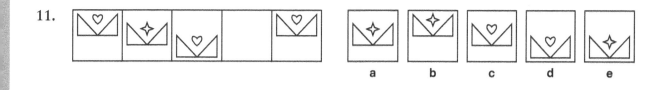

a b c d e

12.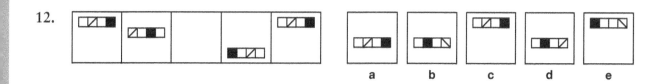

a b c d e

In each question below, there are two shapes or patterns on the left which are similar in some way. Decide how they are similar. Find which of the five shapes on the right is most like the two shapes. Mark it on the answer sheet.

Here is an example to help you.

Example

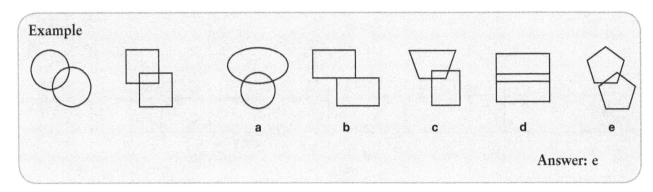

Answer: e

Now try these practice questions.

P1.

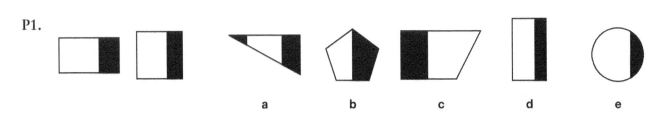

P2.

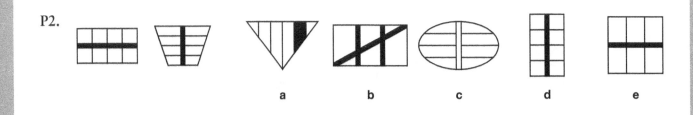

P3.

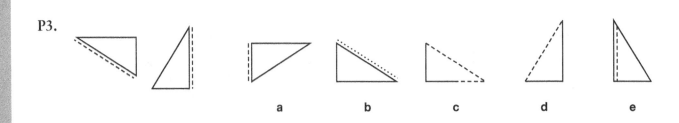

1.

a   b   c   d   e

2.

a   b   c   d   e

3.

a   b   c   d   e

4.

a   b   c   d   e

5.

a   b   c   d   e

6.

a   b   c   d   e

7.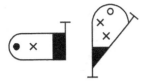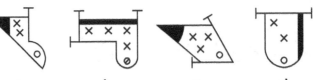

                          a   **b**   **c**   **d**   **e**

8.

                          a   **b**   **c**   **d**   **e**

9.

                          a   **b**   **c**   **d**   **e**

10.

                          a   **b**   **c**   **d**   **e**

11.

                          a   **b**   **c**   **d**   **e**

12.

                          a   **b**   **c**   **d**   **e**

Non-Verbal Reasoning

Multiple-Choice
Practice Test C

Read these instructions carefully.

1. You must not open or turn over this booklet until you are told to do so.

2. The booklet contains a multiple-choice test, in which you have to mark your answer to each question on the separate answer sheet.

3. There are five sections in this test. Each section starts with an explanation of what to do, followed by one or two examples. Explanations of the answers for these are included on the answer sheet. You will then be asked to do some practice questions.

4. You should indicate one answer only for each question by drawing a firm pencil line clearly through the rectangle next to your answer on the answer sheet. Rub out any mistakes as well as you can and put in your new answer.

5. Complete the questions as quickly and carefully as you can. If you find that you cannot do a question, do not waste time on it but go on to the next one.

6. You should do any rough working on a separate sheet of paper.

Section 1

In each of the questions below, there is a sequence of squares with one square left empty. Look at the five squares on the right and find the one that should take the place of the empty square to complete the sequence. Mark it on your answer sheet.

Here is an example to help you.

Example

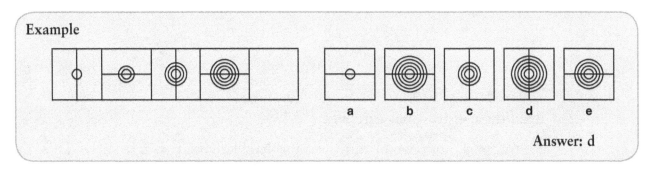

Answer: d

Now try these practice questions.

P1.

P2.

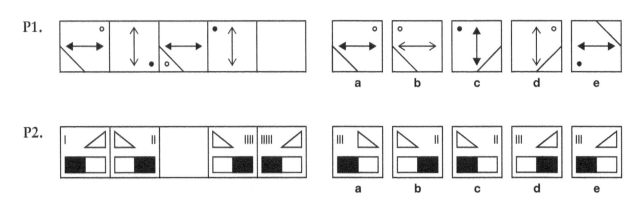

WAIT UNTIL YOU ARE TOLD TO GO ON

1.

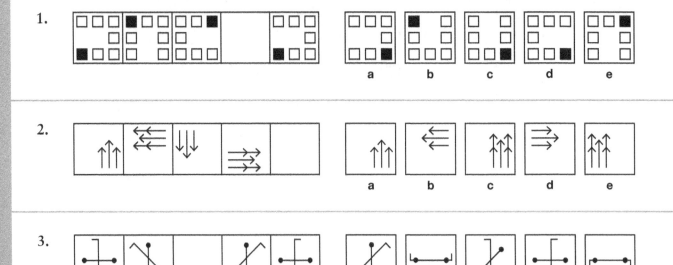

2.

3.

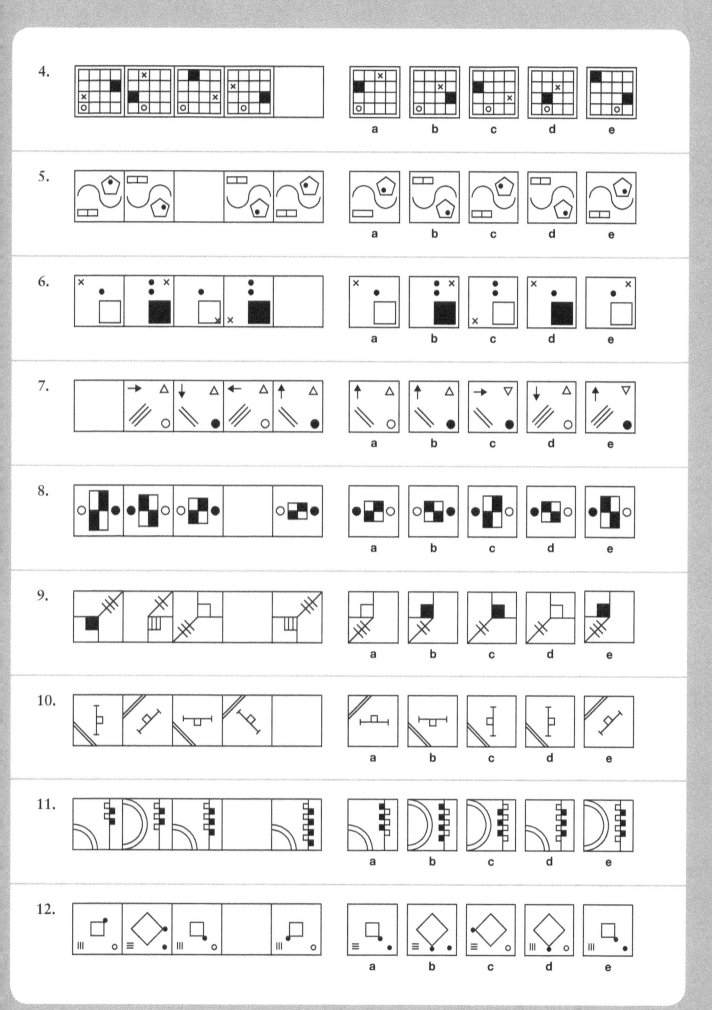

In the grids below, one square has been left empty. Look carefully at the five squares to the right and select the square that should complete the grid. Mark it on your answer sheet.

Here is an example to help you.

Example

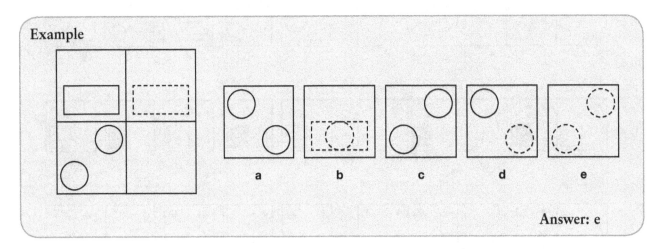

Answer: e

Now try these practice questions.

P1.

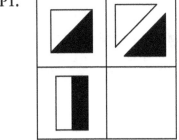   

a   b   c   d   e

P2.

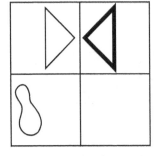    

a   b   c   d   e

P3.

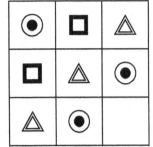

a   b   c   d   e

P4.

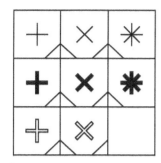

a	b	c	d	e

WAIT UNTIL YOU ARE TOLD TO GO ON

1.

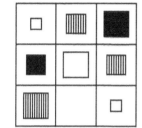

a   b   c   d   e

2.

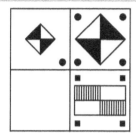

a   b   c   d   e

3.

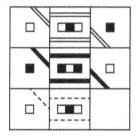

a   b   c   d   e

4.

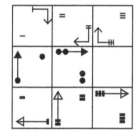

a   b   c   d   e

5.

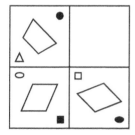

a   b   c   d   e

NOW GO ON TO THE NEXT PAGE

6.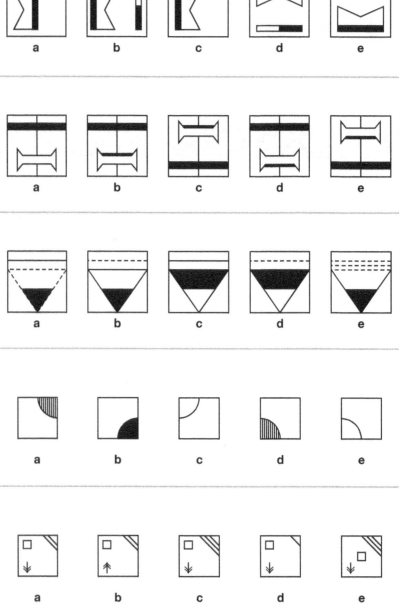

        a   b   c   d   e

7.

        a   b   c   d   e

8.

        a   b   c   d   e

9.

        a   b   c   d   e

10.

        a   b   c   d   e

11.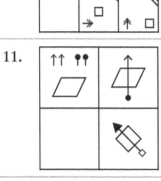

        a   b   c   d   e

12.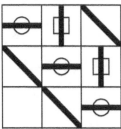

        a   b   c   d   e

Section 3

In each of the questions below, there are two shapes on the left with an arrow between them. Look at them carefully and decide how the second shape is related to the first shape. There is then a third shape and another arrow followed by five more shapes. Decide which of the five shapes completes the second pair in the same way as the first pair. Mark it on your answer sheet.

Here is an example to help you.

Example

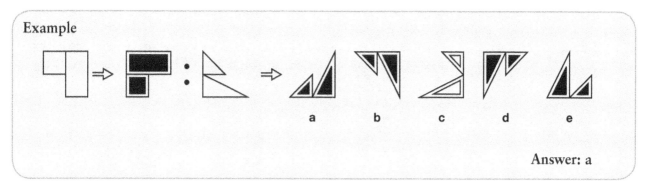

Answer: a

Now try these practice questions.

P1.
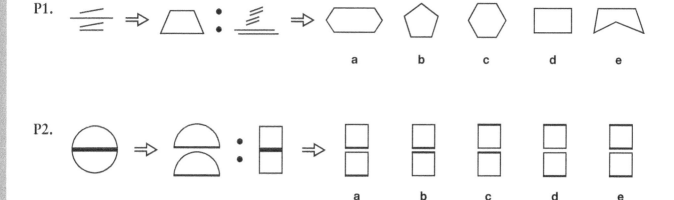

P2.

WAIT UNTIL YOU ARE TOLD TO GO ON

1.
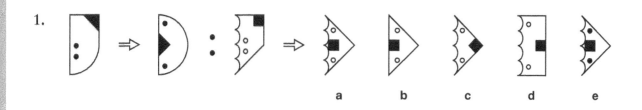

2.
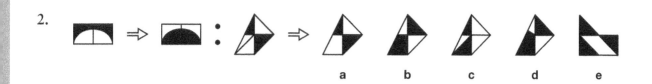

3.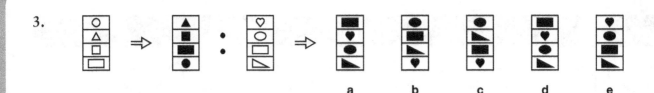

a b c d e

4.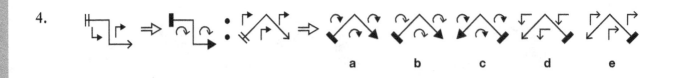

a b c d e

5.

a b c d e

6.

a b c d e

7.

a b c d e

8.

a   b   c   d   e

9.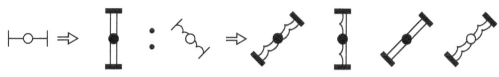

a   b   c   d   e

10.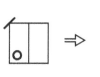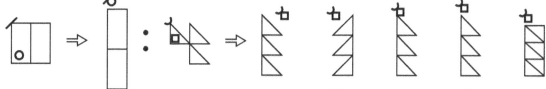

a   b   c   d   e

11.

a   b   c   d   e

12.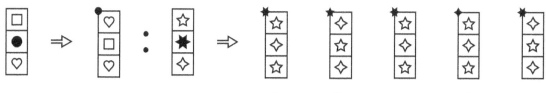

a   b   c   d   e

In the questions below, you have to work out a code. You are given some shapes and the codes that go with them. Decide how the codes match the shapes. Then look at the test shape and find its correct code from the five given on the right. Mark it on your answer sheet.

Here are two examples to help you.

Look at Example 1.

Example 1

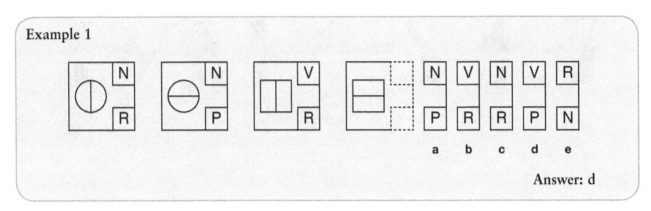

a   b   c   d   e

Answer: d

The top letter is for the shape, with N for circle and V for square.
The lower letter is for the orientation of the line, with R for vertical and P for horizontal.
So the code for the square with a horizontal line is VP, which is option **d**.

Now look at Example 2.

Example 2

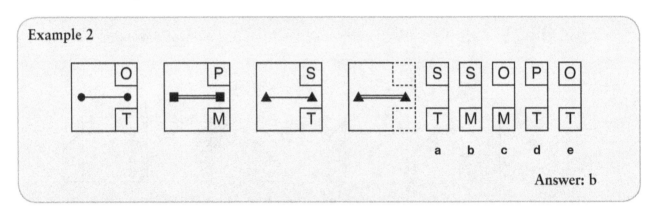

a   b   c   d   e

Answer: b

In this example, the top letter is for the shapes on either end of the line, with O for circles, P for squares and S for triangles.
The lower letter is for the type of line, with T for single and M for double.
So the code for the double line with triangles is SM, which is option **b**.

Now try these practice questions.

P1.

a   b   c   d   e

P2.

a   b   c   d   e

P3.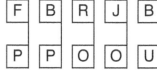

a   b   c   d   e

WAIT UNTIL YOU ARE TOLD TO GO ON

1.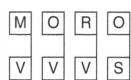

a   b   c   d   e

2.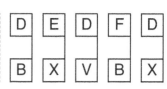

a   b   c   d   e

3.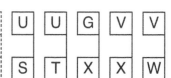

a   b   c   d   e

4.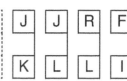

a   b   c   d   e

5.

a   b   c   d   e

6.

	a	b	c	d	e
top	A	B	T	H	B
bottom	W	E	W	D	D

7.

	a	b	c	d	e
top	R	Y	Q	Y	R
bottom	O	O	P	P	P

8.

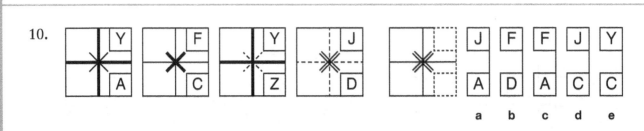

	a	b	c	d	e
top	G	A	C	K	G
bottom	I	V	V	L	V

9.

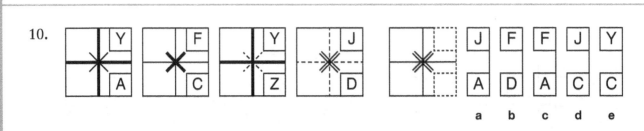

	a	b	c	d	e
top	C	T	B	C	T
bottom	J	F	F	Q	Q

10.

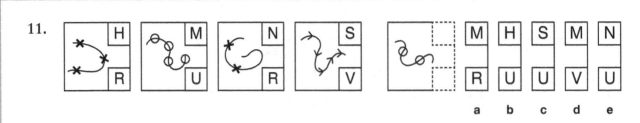

	a	b	c	d	e
top	J	F	F	J	Y
bottom	A	D	A	C	C

11.

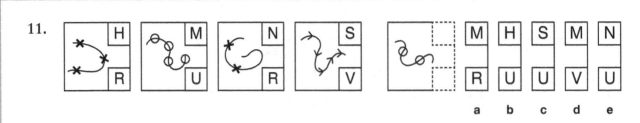

	a	b	c	d	e
top	M	H	S	M	N
bottom	R	U	U	V	U

12.

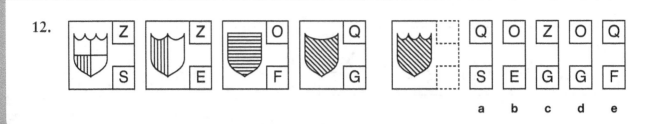

	a	b	c	d	e
top	Q	O	Z	O	Q
bottom	S	E	G	G	F

Section 5

The following questions are about finding the odd one out in a series of shapes or patterns. Find the odd one out and mark it on your answer sheet.

Here is an example to help you.

Example

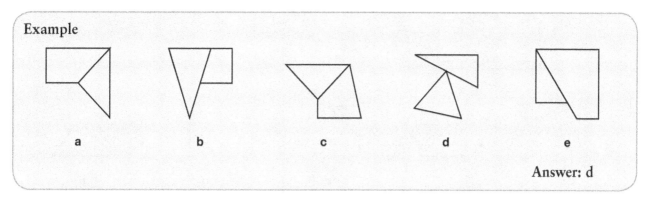

a   b   c   d   e

Answer: d

Now try these practice questions.

P1.

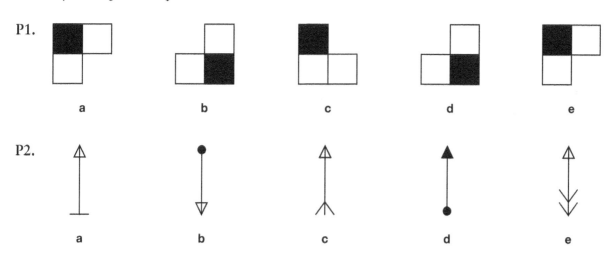

P2.

a   b   c   d   e

WAIT UNTIL YOU ARE TOLD TO GO ON

1.

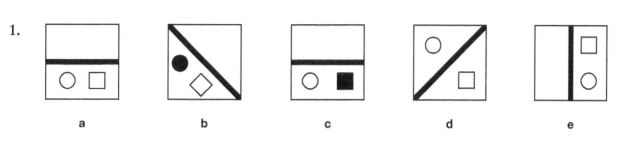

a   b   c   d   e

2.

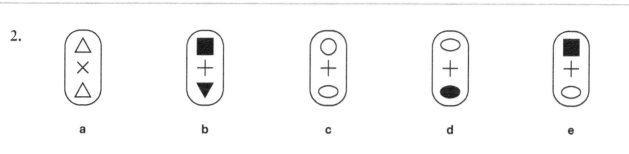

a   b   c   d   e

3.

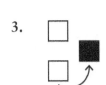

a   b   c   d   e

4.

a   b   c   d   e

5.

a   b   c   d   e

6.

a   b   c   d   e

7.

a   b   c   d   e

8.

a   b   c   d   e

9.

a   b   c   d   e

10.

a   b   c   d   e

11.

a   b   c   d   e

12.

a   b   c   d   e

TEST ADVICE

This information will not appear in the actual test.
It is included here to remind you not to stop working
until you are told the test is over.

CHECK YOUR ANSWERS AGAIN IF THERE IS TIME

CORRECTING EVEN ONE MISTAKE CAN MEAN AN EXTRA MARK

Non-Verbal Reasoning
Multiple-Choice
Practice Test D

Read these instructions carefully.

1. You must not open or turn over this booklet until you are told to do so.

2. The booklet contains a multiple-choice test, in which you have to mark your answer to each question on the separate answer sheet.

3. There are five sections in this test. Each section starts with an explanation of what to do, followed by one or two examples. Explanations of the answers for these are included on the answer sheet. You will then be asked to do some practice questions.

4. You should indicate one answer only for each question by drawing a firm pencil line clearly through the rectangle next to your answer on the answer sheet. Rub out any mistakes as well as you can and put in your new answer.

5. Complete the questions as quickly and carefully as you can. If you find that you cannot do a question, do not waste time on it but go on to the next one.

6. You should do any rough working on a separate sheet of paper.

Section 1

In the grids below, one square has been left empty. Look carefully at the five squares to the right and select the square that should complete the grid. Mark it on your answer sheet.

Here is an example to help you.

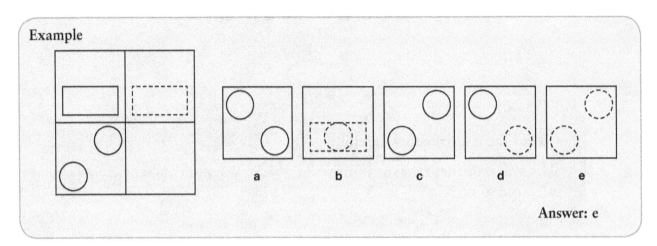

Example

Answer: e

Now try these practice questions.

P1.

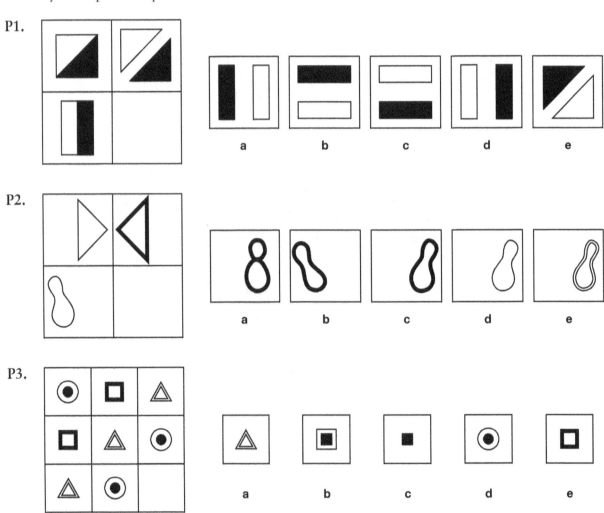

P2.

P3.

P4.

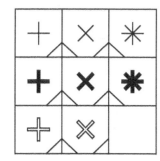

      a   b   c   d   e

WAIT UNTIL YOU ARE TOLD TO GO ON

1.

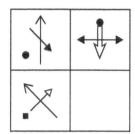

      a   b   c   d   e

2.

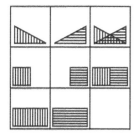

      a   b   c   d   e

3.

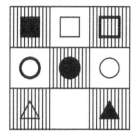

      a   b   c   d   e

4.

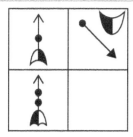

      a   b   c   d   e

5.

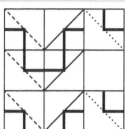

      a   b   c   d   e

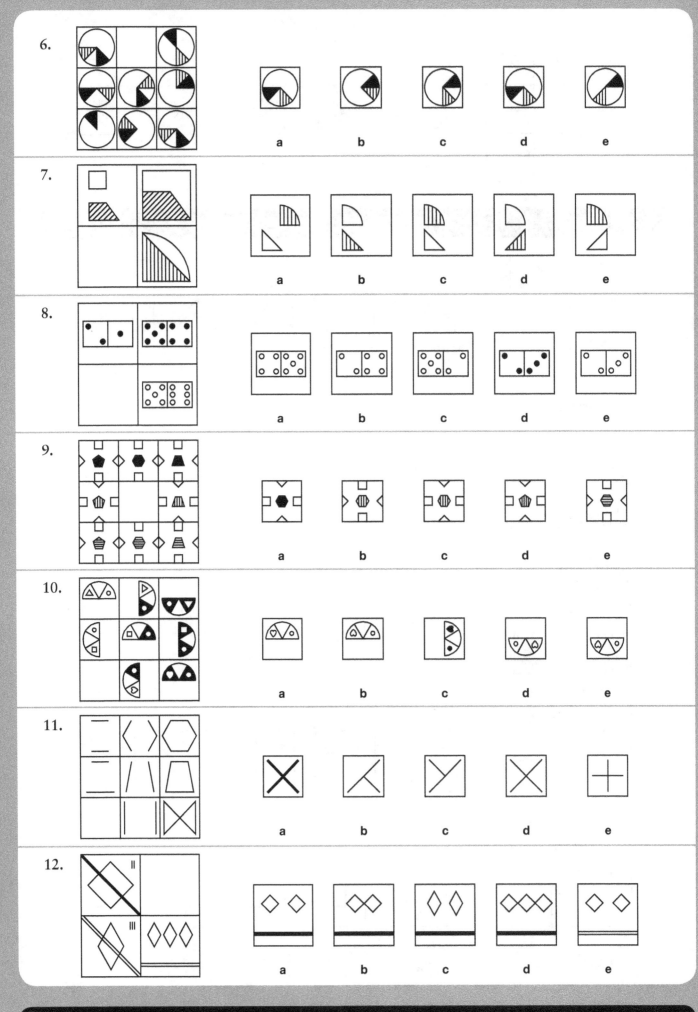

6.   a   b   c   d   e

7.   a   b   c   d   e

8.   a   b   c   d   e

9.   a   b   c   d   e

10.   a   b   c   d   e

11.   a   b   c   d   e

12.   a   b   c   d   e

Section 2

In each of the questions below, there are two shapes on the left with an arrow between them. Look at them carefully and decide how the second shape is related to the first shape. There is then a third shape and another arrow followed by five more shapes. Decide which of the five shapes completes the second pair in the same way as the first pair. Mark it on your answer sheet.

Here is an example to help you.

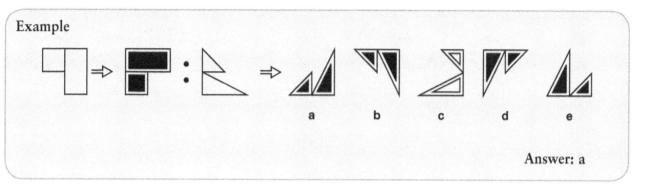

Example

a   b   c   d   e

Answer: a

Now try these practice questions.

P1.

a   b   c   d   e

P2.

a   b   c   d   e

WAIT UNTIL YOU ARE TOLD TO GO ON

1.

a   b   c   d   e

2.

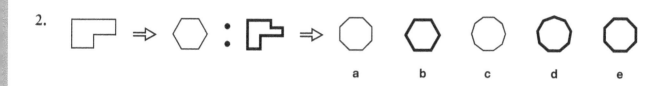

a   b   c   d   e

3.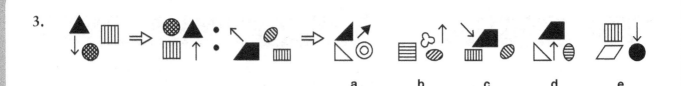

             a   b   c   d   e

4.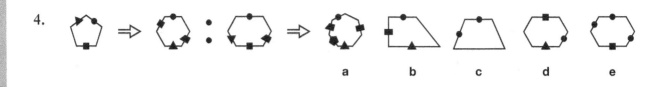

             a   b   c   d   e

5.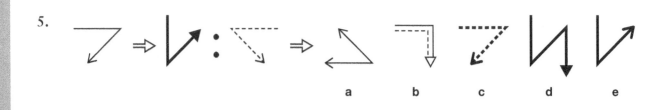

             a   b   c   d   e

6.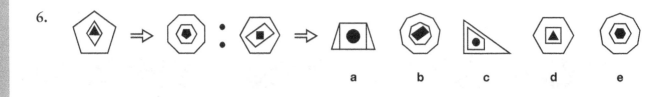

             a   b   c   d   e

7.

             a   b   c   d   e

8.

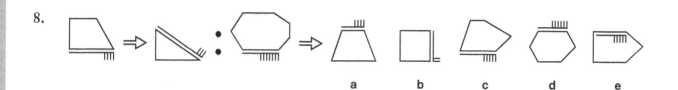

                                              a   b   c   d   e

9.

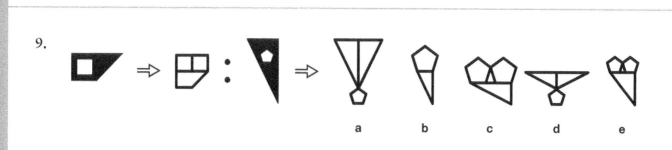

                                              a   b   c   d   e

10.

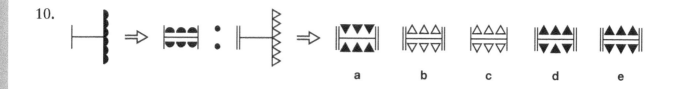

                                              a   b   c   d   e

11.

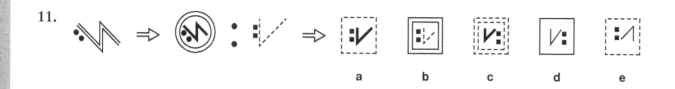

                                              a   b   c   d   e

12.

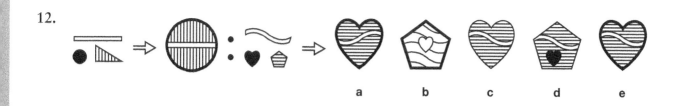

                                              a   b   c   d   e

Section 3

In each of the questions below, there is a sequence of squares with one square left empty. Look at the five squares on the right and find the one that should take the place of the empty square to complete the sequence. Mark it on your answer sheet.

Here is an example to help you.

Example

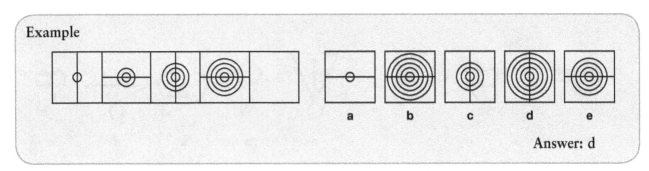

Answer: d

Now try these practice questions.

P1.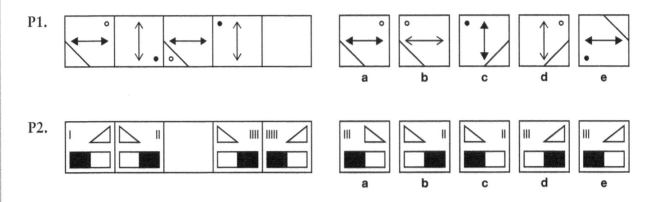

P2.

WAIT UNTIL YOU ARE TOLD TO GO ON

1.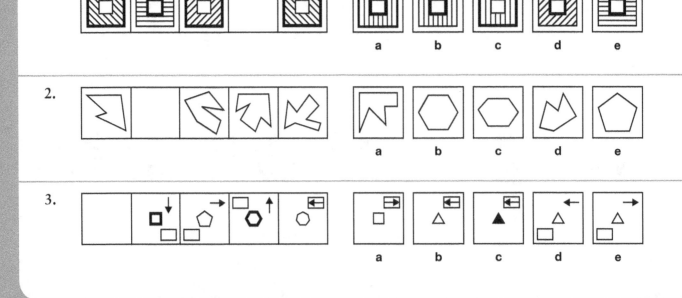

2.

3.

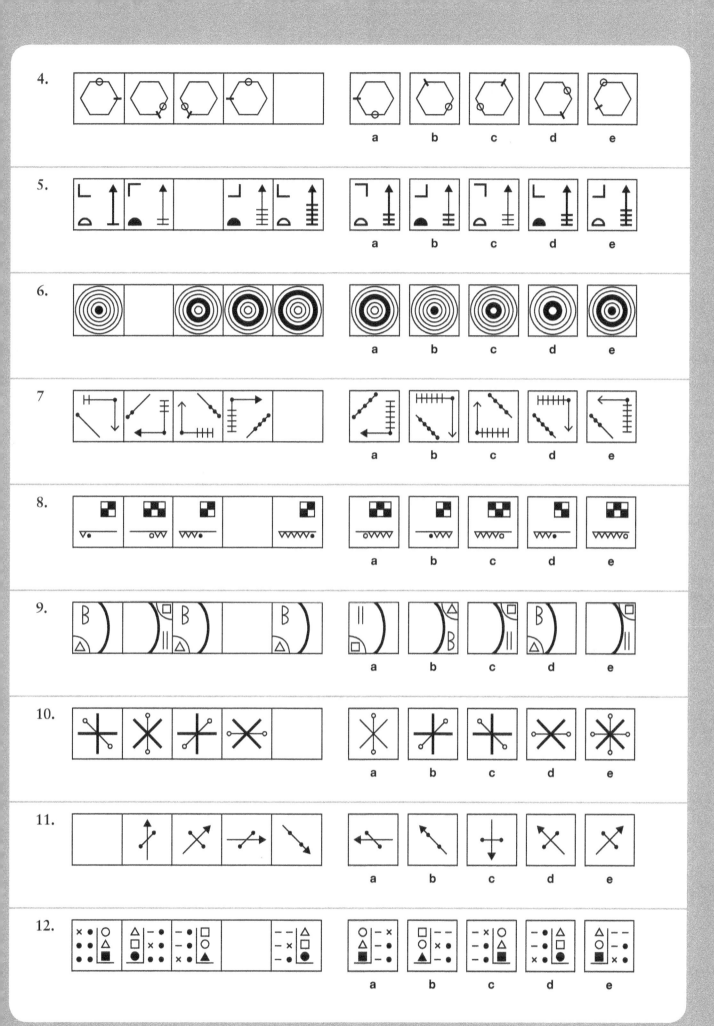

The following questions are about finding the odd one out in a series of shapes or patterns. Find the odd one out and mark it on your answer sheet.

Here is an example to help you.

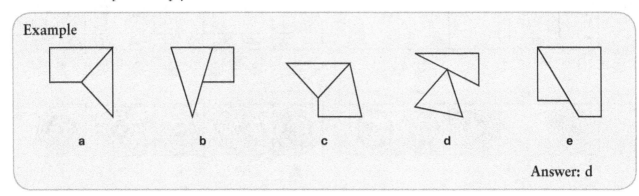

Example

a   b   c   d   e

Answer: d

Now try these practice questions.

P1.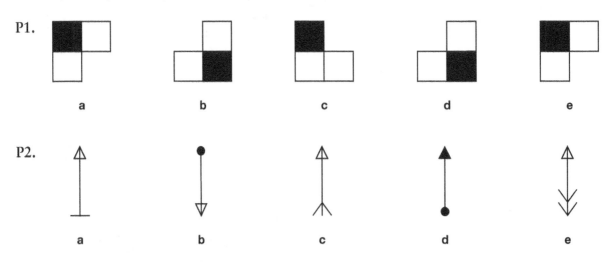

a   b   c   d   e

P2.

a   b   c   d   e

WAIT UNTIL YOU ARE TOLD TO GO ON

1.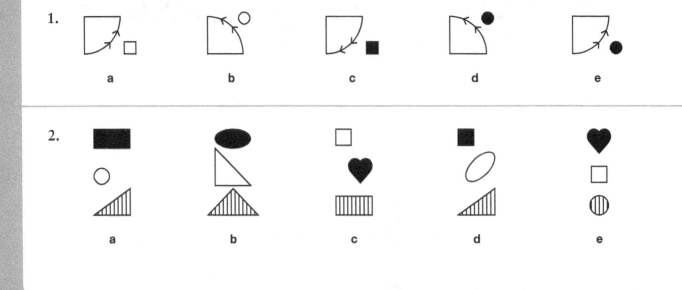

a   b   c   d   e

2.

a   b   c   d   e

3.

a

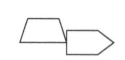
b

c

d

e

4.

a

b

c

d

e

5.

a

b

c

d

e

6.

a

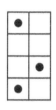
b

c

d

e

7.

a

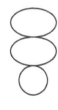
b

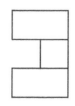
c

d

e

NOW GO ON TO THE NEXT PAGE

8.

a   b   c   d   e

9.

a   b   c   d   e

10.

a   b   c   d   e

11.

a   b   c   d   e

12.

a   b   c   d   e

In the questions below, you have to work out a code. You are given some shapes and the codes that go with them. Decide how the codes match the shapes. Then look at the test shape and find its correct code from the five given on the right. Mark it on your answer sheet.

Here are two examples to help you.

Look at Example 1.

Example 1

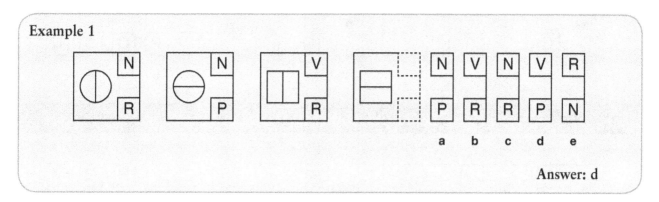

Answer: d

The top letter is for the shape, with N for circle and V for square.
The lower letter is for the orientation of the line, with R for vertical and P for horizontal.
So the code for the square with a horizontal line is VP, which is option **d**.

Now look at Example 2.

Example 2

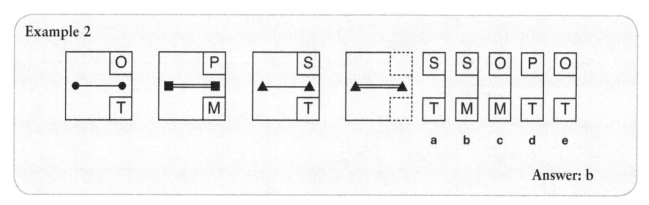

Answer: b

In this example, the top letter is for the shapes on either end of the line, with O for circles, P for squares and S for triangles.
The lower letter is for the type of line, with T for single and M for double.
So the code for the double line with triangles is SM, which is option **b**.

Now try these practice questions.

P1.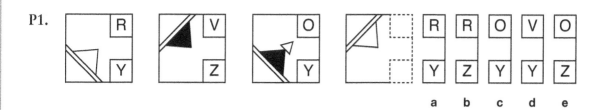

P2.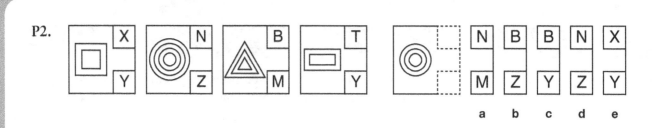

P3.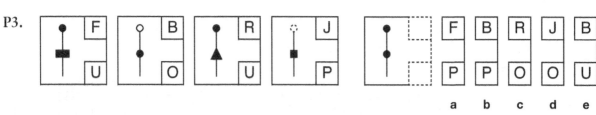

WAIT UNTIL YOU ARE TOLD TO GO ON

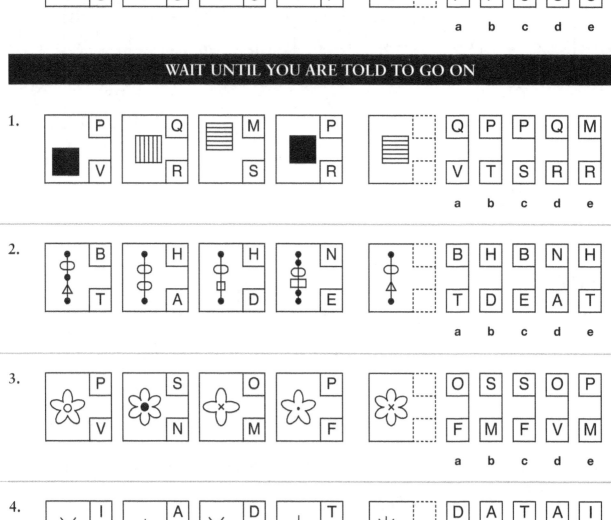

NOW GO ON TO THE NEXT PAGE

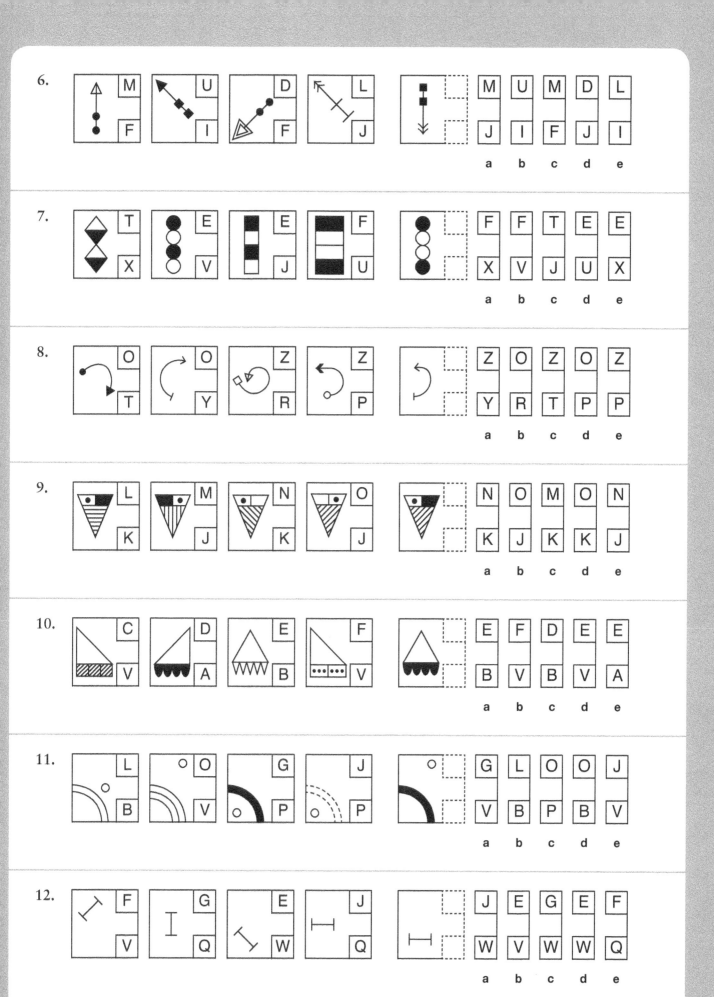

TEST ADVICE

This information will not appear in the actual test.
It is included here to remind you not to stop working
until you are told the test is over.

CHECK YOUR ANSWERS AGAIN IF THERE IS TIME

CORRECTING EVEN ONE MISTAKE CAN MEAN AN EXTRA MARK

Collins

PRACTICE PAPERS

Answers and Explanations

Non-Verbal Reasoning

Marking

Award one mark for each correct answer. Half marks are not allowed, and marks are not given for 'very nearly correct answers'. No marks are deducted for wrong answers.

If scores are low, look at the paper and identify which question types seem to be harder for your child. Then spend some time going over them together. If your child is very accurate and gets correct answers, but works too slowly, try getting them to do one of the practice papers with time targets going through. If you are helpful and look for ways to help your child, they will grow in confidence and feel well prepared when they take the actual examinations.

Practice Test A Answers and Explanations

Section 1
E.g. d
Line bisecting the square alternates vertically/horizontally; concentric circle gains 1 extra circle in each box.

P1. a
Arrow direction alternates; arrowhead alternates; dot colour alternates; dot moves 90° clockwise; alternate boxes have diagonal line across bottom left-hand corner.

P2. e
The triangle and rectangle reflect in each box; number of lines increases by 1 and their position is reflected.

1. e
Semicircle moves 45° clockwise; bold line alternates between top and bottom; dots and crosses alternate.

2. a
Shading moves upwards by 1 rectangle.

3. e
Arrows alternate; number of lines on arrow increases by 1 in every other box; dot colour and direction of short, diagonal line alternate.

4. a
Presence of double arm alternates; other arm rotates 135° clockwise.

5. b
Position of 'square' alternates; shading alternates between vertical stripes, horizontal stripes and dots.

6. d
Bold lines rotate 90° clockwise; bold cross remains the same; number of dots increases by 1.

7. e
Two figures alternate.

8. a
T-shape rotates 90° clockwise; line with dot rotates 45° clockwise, remaining in the same position relative to the T-shape.

9. b
Chevrons rotate 90° clockwise, increasing by 1 alternate dark/light line each time.

10. c
Cross with 1 side joined rotates 90° clockwise; dot colour alternates; arrow alternates up/down; 'star' gains 1 point.

11. b
End lines alternate; line of triangles rotates 135° clockwise.

12. a
Long line rotates 45° clockwise; extra perpendicular short line added every other box; number of dots increases by 1; colour of dots alternates.

Section 2
E.g. e
Identical shapes overlapping to bottom right of the upper shape.

P1. d
Shapes with the right-hand third shaded.

P2. d
Shapes divided into eight with a bold line down the centre.

P3. a
Triangles with a parallel dashed line on the outside of 1 side.

1. d
Shapes divided into 4 with a small, dark concentric shape in 1 quarter.

2. d
Shapes have a longer bold line and shorter fine line perpendicular to the outline.

3. b
Shapes have 1 bold side and 1 dot inside and 2 dots outside, next to one another.

4. b
Pentagons with 2 parallel lines inside, 1 curved shaded corner and 2 short parallel lines intersecting 1 edge.

5. d
Number of lines parallel to edges outside the shapes is the same as the number of crosses inside.

6. a
Right-angled arrows with a dot at the corner, double parallel perpendicular lines on the arrowhead side of the arrow and a single perpendicular line on the opposite end to the arrowhead.

7. c
Figures consist of a dark quadrilateral, star and circle. Circle has the same number of dots around it as there are points on the star. Shapes do not touch.

8. c
Rectangles divided vertically in half, with small triangles to left and small squares to right. Same number of vertical lines in centre as total number of small shapes.

9. b
Same number of curved sides as there are dashed rectangles outside the large shape.

10. a
Taller shape on the left-hand side, adjacent to shorter version of the same shape on right.

11. e
Clockwise arrows.

12. a
1 corner marked off with straight line, elongated 'H' shape bisecting 1 corner.

Section 3
E.g. a
Shape rotates 90° anticlockwise; smaller dark identical shapes added inside each section.

P1. a
Lines are arranged into a shape.

P2. a

Shape is divided in half horizontally, bottom half rotates and the shapes are aligned vertically.

1. c

Upper small rectangle is moved to the opposite, inner, lower side of the large square; lower rectangle remains the same.

2. c

External shape is rotated 180° and elongated; upper line remains the same and lower line is doubled.

3. a

Figure is rotated 90° clockwise.

4. b

Number of small shapes doubles; central shape gains diagonal shading from bottom left to top right.

5. d

Figure gains additional outer dashed concentric line; inner line becomes dashed.

6. d

Figure gains additional set of perpendicular lines; dashed line extends all the way around; figure rotated 180°.

7. a

Arrow rotated 90° clockwise; double-lined part becomes bold; clear arrowhead becomes filled and is swapped with the double perpendicular lines.

8. b

Dashed and solid lines composing the large shapes are swapped; the colour of the small shapes is swapped.

9. b

Arrow changes to become short perpendicular arrows (same number as there are short perpendicular lines on the left-hand figure). The direction of the new arrows match the direction of the original arrow.

10. d

Shape is rotated 90° anticlockwise and the style of the outer and inner arrows is swapped.

11. a

The two shapes at each end of the line are moved together and the dark and white shading swapped; the horizontal line style becomes the outline style of the new shape formed.

12. a

A touching mirror image is added with dark shading.

Section 4

E.g. e

Moving left to right, shapes become dashed.

P1. d

Moving left to right, the two halves of the shape separate.

P2. c

Moving left to right, the shape is reflected and made bold.

P3. e

Diagonally from bottom left to top right, each line of shapes is identical; they are repeated in turn.

P4. e

Figures in the third column are a combination of the figures in the first two columns; third column has short line across corner in bottom left.

1. d

Moving left to right, the figure is reflected above and the colours are reversed. The colours are unchanged in the original shape.

2. d

Moving left to right, the lines crossing the corners are moved 1 corner anticlockwise; dark shapes around the white circles are doubled and arranged above 4 white circles.

3. e

Moving left to right, the dark section moves 45° anticlockwise; size of circles alters from large, to medium, to small.

4. b

Moving left to right, curved cornered rectangle rotated 45° anticlockwise; arrows moved underneath the rectangle and become double-ended.

5. a

The line in the first column is doubled perpendicularly and combined with the shape in the second column in which the double lines become bold lines.

6. c

Moving right to left, the shapes are reflected and the direction of the stripes is swapped between the two shapes.

7. c

Moving left to right, the arrows are rotated 135° anticlockwise and made shorter, both the same length; dots are added at the opposite ends of the arrows from the arrowheads.

8. b

In each row, the protrusion of the kidney shape should be left, right and inverted, so that each row and column contains one of each type of kidney shape. The type of line is consistent in each row and there are 2 dots with lines through and 1 cross in each row (in top left, top right and bottom right corners).

9. d

Curve rotates 45 degrees clockwise in each row; all small shapes are identical in each column.

10. a

In each row there is a left-pointing quadrilateral, a right-pointing quadrilateral and 2 small quadrilaterals. Each row and column has 1 central, 1 upper and 1 lower figure(s).

11. a

Moving left to right, block of small shapes is rotated 180° and moved to the top of the square; large shape reflected underneath and the original and reflection move to the bottom of the square.

12. b

Each row and column has 1 striped, 1 dark and 1 white circle; there is 1 bold line positioned at the top, centre and bottom of the square in each row; the stripes always run diagonally from bottom left to top right.

Section 5

E.g. 1. a

H stands for a white shape, B for dark and A for striped.

E.g. 2. b

B stands for white shading; Q for dark shading; T stands for diagonally aligned triangles; W for horizontal; R for one upwards and one downwards.

P1. c

Bold line = R; horizontal line at bottom of vertical lines = N: RN

P2. e

White circle = W; pentagon = Z: WZ

1. e

White scallops = R; horizontal lines = G: RG

2. c

Hearts = I; shapes at top = C: IC

3. a

White sector = R; dark sector = V: RV

4. c

Square divided horizontally/vertically = H; 3 circles = T; 1 cross = C: HTC

5. d

Rhombus = Y; 4 corners shaded = G: YG

6. e

T-shape pointing right = R; white swirl = A; white pentagon = U: RAU

7. a

2 dots = S; 2 dark sections = F: SF

8. a

Clear square = O; 2 white and 1 dark raindrop = R; dark dot = C: ORC

9. b

Scallops = R; top and bottom shape only shaded = Z; perpendicular line at left-hand side = X: RZX

10. a

L = triangle; W = butterfly-shaped cross: LW

11. a

F = arrow pointing top left; L = upside-down U-shape; V = squares: FLV

12. d

K = 5-point star; Q = dark line; W = no perpendicular lines at either side: KQW

Practice Test B Answers and Explanations

Section 1

E.g. a
Shape rotates 90° anticlockwise; smaller dark identical shapes added inside each section.

P1. a
Lines are arranged into a shape.

P2. a
Shape is divided in half horizontally, bottom half rotates and the shapes are aligned vertically.

1. e
Shape rotates 45° clockwise; clear shapes move to top of line and closer together.

2. b
Shading in sections of shape is reversed.

3. d
Triangle moves to bottom of line; line becomes bold; the two dark shapes are arranged vertically on the line; the clear shape at the bottom of the line disappears.

4. a
Pentagon rotates 90° anticlockwise; the circles on the outside do not rotate but move apart; the circles on the inside disappear.

5. e
Dark turns white; bold dots change to fine; horizontal stripe turns vertical; diagonal stripe swaps direction.

6. a
Shape cut in half horizontally; two halves placed touching in same alignment as bottom half.

7. a
The number of bold arrows equals the number of sides in the large shape, arranged into a single row and rotated 90° anticlockwise from the original arrow.

8. e
Large shape is reflected horizontally and changes colour; small shape is doubled vertically on right-hand side; surrounding circle has arrowhead in opposite direction.

9. b
The white arrow is moved to the corner of the black arrow so one runs horizontally at the top of the shape; both arrowheads are black; number of sides of the shape increase from 6 to 8.

10. a
Vertical lines become bold; horizontal and diagonal lines become dashed.

11. e
Long arrow turns 90° anticlockwise; short arrow turns 45° anticlockwise.

12. e
Small shapes move 1 place to the right; then those at either end are doubled.

Section 2

E.g. e
Moving left to right, shapes become dashed.

P1. d
Moving left to right, the two halves of the shape separate.

P2. c
Moving left to right, the shape is reflected and made bold.

P3. e
Diagonally from bottom left to top right, each line of shapes is identical; they are repeated in turn.

P4. e
Figures in the third column are a combination of the figures in the first two columns; third column has short line across corner in bottom left.

1. a
Moving left to right, the dark shapes, enlarged, move to the sides of the square and the white shape is enlarged at the top.

2. e
Moving right to left, each shape in the row has 1 additional side; the number of circles decreases by 1.

3. b
Moving left to right, the circle moves 2 corners clockwise and the dark dot 1 corner anticlockwise.

4. c
Striped square moves diagonally across to the opposite corner; position of small shapes reflects to other side; colours are swapped.

5. d
Chevron rotates 1 side clockwise in each row; in each column/row there is a dot, circle with dot and 2 concentric circles with dot.

6. c
Diagonally from top left to bottom right, the figures are identical.

7. b
The right column is the vertical reflection of the left column.

8. a
Moving right to left, the dashed shape becomes dark, the dark shape becomes dashed and the white shape with the solid outline is rotated 90° anticlockwise. The original solid shape moves upwards and to the right, the original dashed shape moves to the bottom right and the original solid line shape rotates and moves to the top left.

9. b
Diagonally top left to bottom right, shapes are identical; diagonally from bottom left to top right, shading is identical.

10. b
Moving from right to left, the curve is reflected diagonally and the thickness is swapped; the vertical line is fine in the top squares and bold in the bottom squares.

11. c
Moving from right to left, the 'T' shape is rotated 180° and the small shapes are swapped.

12. e
The third column consists of shapes from the first column, with alternate sections shaded. The top central section is white.

Section 3

E.g. 1.a
H stands for a white shape, B for dark and A for striped.

E.g. 2.b
B stands for white shading; Q for dark shading; T stands for diagonally aligned triangles; W for horizontal; R for one upwards and one downwards.

P1. c
Bold line = R; patterned line at bottom of vertical lines = N: RN

P2. e
White circle = W; pentagon = Z: WZ

1. a
Bold vertical sides = V; rectangles = A: VA

2. d
Right angle pointing to top left = H; curved dark section = M: HM

3. a
Dark shading top and bottom = S; 3 crosses = U: SU

4. a
Horizontal shading = B; hearts = R; dark oval = U: BRU

5. d
   Semicircle facing right = D; triangle pointing right = Q;
   dashed line = W: DQW
6. a
   Pentagon = L; white triangle = E: LE
7. b
   Dot inside pentagon = Y; cross inside pentagon = P: YP
8. d
   Dot not touching side of rectangle = P; 3 lines = N: PN
9. a
   Bold diagonal line = N; fine circle = K; dark triangle = D:
   NKD
10. b
    Rectangle = F; bold-outlined circle = N: FN
11. a
    Shape in top half of square = V; dark shape = B; small
    square = N: VBN
12. d
    Dark triangle = W; vertically striped rectangle = Y; triangle
    behind rectangle = B: WYB

Section 4

E.g. d
   Line bisecting the square alternates vertically/horizontally;
   concentric circle gains 1 extra circle in each box.
P1. a
   Arrow direction alternates; arrowhead alternates; dot
   colour alternates; dot moves 90° clockwise; alternate boxes
   have diagonal line across bottom left-hand corner.
P2. e
   The triangle and rectangle reflect in each box; number of
   lines increases by 1 and their position is reflected.
1. e
   Striped shading rotates 45° clockwise in each box; rectangle
   rotates 90°/alternates orientation in each box with stripes
   perpendicular to the stripes in the background.
2. c
   White square alternates between top and bottom left-hand
   corners; bold square moves 1 corner clockwise; striped
   triangle alternates between horizontal and vertical shading;
   the triangle is reflected diagonally for each pair of figures.
3. e
   Narrow and wide bands to the left-hand side alternate;
   dashed shapes alternate between triangle, rectangle
   and oval.
4. a
   Rectangle alternates between vertical and horizontal;
   number of circles alternates; arrow gains alternately another
   arrowhead and another perpendicular line at base.
5. d
   Orientation of lines and triangles alternates; number of
   circles increases by 1 in each square.
6. a
   Rectangle rotates 45° anticlockwise in each square; scallops
   alternate between top and bottom of square, and between
   colour; small shapes move 1 position left in each figure.
7. e
   Moving left to right, the small dark shape becomes the
   outer shape in the following square. The inner shapes are
   the next outer shape.
8. a
   Arrow moves 90° clockwise around the square in each
   figure; arrowhead moves to the other end of arrow in
   each figure.

9. b
   Line across corner moves towards centre with each figure;
   elongated 'H' shape rotates 45° clockwise in each figure;
   dot alternates between dark and clear.
10. a
    Clear circle moves 1 rung lower on the ladder in each
    figure; dark dot moves 1 rung higher.
11. a
    Shape alternates between heart and star; triangles alternate
    between upper, middle and lower, then middle and upper
    part of the square.
12. d
    Shading moves 1 square to the left; line of squares moves
    progressively lower then back up to the top.

Section 5

E.g. e
   Identical shapes overlapping in bottom right-hand corner
   of the upper shape.
P1. d
   Shapes with the right-hand third shaded.
P2. d
   Shapes divided into eight with a bold line down the centre.
P3. a
   Triangles with a parallel dashed line on the outside of
   1 side.
1. e
   Number of small dark shapes is the same as the number of
   sides of the large shape.
2. d
   Single shaded corner is opposite the curved side.
3. c
   Scallop has stripes perpendicular to the white elongated
   rectangle; single dark section in the white elongated
   rectangle is small.
4. e
   Right-angled triangles with second-longest side bold.
5. a
   Irregular pentagons.
6. e
   Dashed shape is a copy of the solid shape rotated 180° and
   overlaid on top.
7. d
   Same number of 'T' shapes as there are crosses inside.
8. e
   Quarter circle has triangle touching point-to-point and a
   double line on the curve.
9. d
   Exactly 3 eighths shaded with differing patterns.
10. c
    2 dark eighths only, directly opposite one another.
11. c
    Shape reflected and touching its reflection; one half with
    double line furthest from centre point; dark triangle at
    origin of arrow, pointing to double line.
12. d
    3 concentric shapes, inner one dashed; number of dots in
    centre is half the number of sides of the shapes.

Practice Test C Answers and Explanations

Section 1

E.g. d
Line bisecting the square alternates vertically/horizontally; concentric circle gains 1 extra circle in each box.

P1. a
Arrow direction alternates; arrowhead alternates; dot colour alternates; dot moves 90° clockwise; alternate boxes have diagonal line across bottom left-hand corner.

P2. e
The triangle and rectangle reflect in each box; number of lines increases by 1 and their position is reflected.

1. c
Horseshoe of squares rotates 90° anticlockwise in each figure; dark square moves 1 corner clockwise in each figure.

2. a
Arrows move 1 corner anticlockwise in each figure; arrows alternate between short with 3 arrowheads and long with 5 arrowheads.

3. e
Long line rotates 45° anticlockwise in each figure; short line alternates between vertical and horizontal.

4. a
White dot alternates between bottom left corner and 1 square to the right. From left to right, dark square moves to position of cross in previous figure.

5. e
Two figures alternate; the only change is the position of the dot, which moves 1 corner clockwise in the pentagon each figure.

6. a
Squares alternate between white and dark; number of dots alternates between 1 and 2; cross moves 1 corner clockwise.

7. b
Arrow rotates 90° clockwise in each figure; dot alternates between dark and white; lines alternate between 3 parallel (bottom left to top right) and 2 parallel (top left to bottom right).

8. d
Rectangle becomes shorter vertically in each figure; colours alternate between dark and white in the dots in the sections of each figure.

9. b
Square rotates 1 corner anticlockwise in each figure; colours alternate between dark, striped and white; diagonal line is reflected every second figure; number of perpendicular lines alternates between 2 and 3.

10. c
Double corner lines alternate between top left and bottom left; elongated 'H' shape rotates 45° clockwise in each figure; square alternates between upper and lower side of the 'H'.

11. e
Curves alternate between bottom left and left-hand side; total number of small squares increases by 1 in each figure; white small squares are to the left of the line and dark are to the right.

12. b
Squares alternate between small and large; 3 parallel lines alternate between vertical and horizontal; separate dots alternate between white and dark; dark dot moves 45° clockwise touching the square in each figure.

Section 2

E.g. e
Moving left to right, shapes become dashed.

P1. d
Moving left to right, the two halves of the shape separate.

P2. c
Moving left to right, the shape is reflected and made bold.

P3. e
Diagonally from bottom left to top right, each line of shapes is identical; they are repeated in turn.

P4. e
Figures in the third column are a combination of the figures in the first two columns; third column has short line across corner in bottom left.

1. c
Diagonally bottom left to top right, size of squares consistent; diagonally top left to bottom right, shading of squares consistent.

2. e
Moving from left to right, the size of the shape is increased; the small shape in the bottom right-hand corner is duplicated in all 4 corners; shading in the main shape is reversed.

3. a
In the third column, all lines are in bottom left-hand corner; line style is consistent in each row; each row contains one single white square and one single dark square.

4. c
From right to left in each row, arrow moves 1 side clockwise in each figure and the position of the separate shapes moves 1 corner clockwise. In the third column, there are 3 vertical separate figures and 3 identical shapes at the end of each arrow; all small separate shapes are arranged vertically.

5. e
Moving left to right, the figure is rotated 45° clockwise; the small shapes swap positions and colour.

6. b
The figures are reflected in a vertical mirror line.

7. d
The large shape is reflected horizontally across the centre of the square; a bold horizontal line is added in the original position of the large shape and a fine vertical line down the centre.

8. e
The parallel lines in the top left-hand corner are moved to the top of the figure; the triangles are enlarged and become 1 triangle with the shading matching the upper/lower shading on the left-hand side.

9. e
Diagonally from bottom left to top right, the position of the curve is consistent; diagonally from top left to bottom right, the shading of the curve is consistent.

10. c
From left to right, arrow rotates 90° anticlockwise in each square; each row has a figure with 1, 2 or 3 lines across the top right corner; small shapes in first column are all in top left corner.

11. c
Moving from left to right, the large shape moves up to the centre of the box; arrows on left-hand side give arrowhead for top of arrow; figures on right-hand side give other end of the arrow; arrows are in the same direction.

12. a
Diagonally from top left to bottom right, the figures are all identical.

Section 3

E.g. a
Shape rotates 90° anticlockwise; smaller dark identical shapes added inside each section.

P1. a
Lines are arranged into a shape.

P2. a
Shape is divided in half horizontally, bottom half rotates and the shapes are aligned vertically.

1. a
Small dark shape in top right-hand corner moves to centre of left-hand side of shape; dots separate to top and bottom corners of left-hand side of shape; outline of bottom half of large shape is reflected upwards.

2. b
Colours are reversed.

3. b
Each shape moves 1 rectangle upwards and colour changes to dark.

4. b
Arrowhead of single arrow changes to a dark triangle; double perpendicular lines change to bold single line; small arrows change to curved arrows with fine arrowheads.

5. e
Shape on left becomes 1 corner of square; the arrowhead is the same as the shape of the arrowhead on the left-hand side, and is positioned on the same side of the shape as it is on the arrow.

6. a
Shape is reflected horizontally; colour changes to dark.

7. e
Dark and white curves turn outwards.

8. a
Dashed shape is enlarged slightly and encloses the solid shape; dashed semicircle is added on 1 side of the shape.

9. c
Shape is divided in half horizontally and upper half placed below lower, touching.

10. a
Elongated 'H' shape rotates 90° clockwise; dot changes to dark; both ends of the 'H' shape become bold; centre part of 'H' shape becomes a double line.

11. d
Large shapes are arranged vertically, touching one another; small bold shape is positioned above but not touching; corner shape moves to top left corner of small bold shape, touching.

12. e
Shape in the bottom square is duplicated in the top square; top shape moves into the centre square; centre shape is made smaller and moves to top left-hand corner of grid.

Section 4

E.g. 1.d
The top letter is for the shape, the bottom letter for the dividing line. N stands for circle, V for square; R for vertical dividing line, P for horizontal.

E.g. 2.b
The top letter is for the shapes on either side of the line, the bottom for the single or double line. O stands for circles, P for squares, S for triangles; T stands for single line, M for double.

P1. b
White triangle = R; figure in top left = Z: RZ

P2. a
Circles = N; 3 concentric shapes = M: NM

P3. e
Dark circle in the centre = B; dark circle at top = U: BU

1. e
1 dark section = R; shape divided into 4 squares = N: RN

2. a
Fine arrowhead = D; single bold line at top = b: DB

3. e
Small circle = V; vertical divide = W: VW

4. b
Dark dot on top line = J; clear dot on second from top line = L: JL

5. b
Irregular pentagon = H; 2 bold sides = V: HV

6. b
Dark chevrons = B; spiral = E: BE

7. e
Line at centre of figure = R; zigzag line = P: RP

8. b
2 dark circles = A; 2 triangles = V: AV

9. e
Circles/ovals = T; 4 shapes = Q: TQ

10. b
Fine horizontal/vertical cross = F; double diagonal cross = D: FD

11. e
2 small shapes = N; circles = U: NU

12. a
Diagonal stripe = Q; 3-scallop shield = S: QS

Section 5

E.g. d
The only figure not made up of a quadrilateral and a triangle touching by the sides.

P1. c
The only figure in which the corner square is not shaded.

P2. d
The only figure with a shaded arrowhead.

1. d
The only figure in which the two shapes are on opposite sides of the line.

2. a
The only figure without a '+' sign in the centre.

3. b
The only figure with an arrow pointing to a white square.

4. a
The only figure with 2 corner lines rather than 3.

5. b
The only figure without a line touching a corner.

6. c
The only figure with a double set of perpendicular lines each end of the 'H' shape.

7. d
The other shapes have 1 more side on the inner shape than the outer.

8. b
The other shapes all have anticlockwise arrows.

9. e
The other double lines all cross at right angles.

10. b
The only figure with 2 small shapes that are identical in shape.

11. e
The only figure with a small white shape at the top and a small black shape at the bottom.

12. c
Other figures have 1 dot fewer than there are sections in the rectangle.

Practice Test D Answers and Explanations

Section 1

E.g. e
Moving left to right, shapes become dashed.

P1. d
Moving left to right, the two halves of the shape separate.

P2. c
Moving left to right, the shape is reflected and made bold.

P3. e
Diagonally from bottom left to top right, each line of shapes is identical; they are repeated in turn.

P4. e
Figures in the third column are a combination of the figures in the first two columns; third column has short line across corner in bottom left.

1. c
Moving left to right, the short arrow rotates 45° anticlockwise and becomes double-ended; the long arrow becomes double width and rotates 180°. The small shape moves to the flat end of the long arrow.

2. e
The figures in the third column are those of the first two columns placed directly over one another.

3. b
In each row, there is a bold, fine and solid shape; striped backgrounds alternate.

4. b
Moving left to right, the arrow rotates 135° clockwise and the dots move to the end. The arrow head becomes solid. The shield shape is enlarged, rotated 180° and moved to the top right-hand corner.

5. a
In each row, the bold corner moves 1 place anticlockwise; in each column the diagonal lines are identical.

6. e
In each row, the dark section moves 90° anticlockwise; the striped sections move 45° anticlockwise.

7. b
Moving left to right, the shapes are enlarged and the white shape moves behind the striped shape.

8. e
Moving left to right, each side of the domino gains 3 dots.

9. c
Each column has the same central shape; each row has the same shading and small shapes around the edge.

10. d
In each row, the semicircle is rotated 90° clockwise; in each column, the number of sections shaded is consistent.

11. d
The figures in the first column go together with those in the second column to make those in the third.

12. a
Moving left to right, the large shape becomes smaller and is replicated the same number of times as there are short parallel lines in the top right; the diagonal line becomes horizontal and is moved to the bottom of the square.

Section 2

E.g. a
Shape rotates 90° anticlockwise, smaller dark identical shapes added inside each section.

P1. a
Lines are arranged into a shape.

P2. a
Shape is divided in half horizontally, bottom half rotates and the shapes are aligned vertically.

1. b
Small section with the dot in is shaded; rest of figure is not replicated.

2. e
The number of sides on the left-hand shape is made into a regular polygon.

3. c
Moving left to right, the shapes move but remain the same, the arrow turns to point in the opposite direction, towards the shaded shape.

4. a
Moving left to right, shape gains an additional side. Number of small shapes is 2 fewer than the number of sides.

5. c
Arrow rotated 135° clockwise, made bold and arrowhead swaps side.

6. e
The outer shape gains 3 sides; the inner two shapes each gain 2 sides.

7. b
The U-shape is rotated 90° clockwise and increases in width; rectangles become triangles; circles and hearts are swapped.

8. d
Moving left to right, the number of sides decreases by 1. The longest side has a parallel line next to it, with the same number of perpendicular lines as there are sides of the shape.

9. e
The dark shape is moved under a doubled version of the small white shape.

10. b
The right-hand side of the skewed 'H' shape gives the pattern for the new horizontal sections; the left-hand side gives the pattern for the vertical sections. The left-hand side of the 'H' shape is mirrored so that it is the same on the left and the right-hand side. Half of the smaller shapes on the right-hand side are rotated 90 degrees anticlockwise and aligned centrally above the; the other half are rotated 90 degrees clockwise and aligned centrally below the H.

11. a
The angled line on the left gives the type of line for the enclosing shape on the right; the angled line becomes bold and solid; the small shapes remain to the left of the angled line.

12. e
Dark shape gives large bold shape; striped shape gives direction of stripes; white shape moves to centre of large shape.

Section 3

E.g. d
Line bisecting the square alternates vertically/horizontally; concentric circle gains 1 extra circle in each box.

P1. a
Arrow direction alternates; arrowhead alternates; dot colour alternates; dot moves 90° clockwise; alternate boxes have diagonal line across bottom left-hand corner.

P2. e
The triangle and rectangle reflect in each box; number of lines increases by 1 and their position is reflected.

1. b
Bold/fine large squares alternate; fine/bold small squares alternate; stripes rotate 45° anticlockwise.

2. d
   Number of sides increases by 1 in each figure; shape is irregular and not symmetrical.
3. b
   Arrow rotates 90° anticlockwise; rectangle moves 1 corner clockwise; shape alternates bold/fine and gains an additional side.
4. b
   Circle moves 2 sides clockwise; bold line moves 1 corner clockwise.
5. a
   L-shape rotates 90° clockwise; arrow gains 1 perpendicular line and alternates bold/fine; semicircle alternates dark/white.
6. c
   The dark circle moves 1 ring outwards and the total number of rings remains the same.
7. d
   The arrow moves 1 corner clockwise; arrowheads alternate fine/bold and gain a perpendicular short line in each figure; the number of dots on the separate diagonal line increases by 1 each time; the length of the arrow is consistent throughout the sequence; diagonal line moves one corner clockwise.
8. a
   The square and rectangle alternate; the number of triangles increases by 1 and they alternate between left and right; the dot alternates dark/white.
9. c
   The two figures alternate.
10. c
    The bold cross alternates vertically/horizontally and diagonally; the line with a dot at each end rotates 45° clockwise.
11. b
    The arrow rotates 45° clockwise; the line with a dot at each end alternates between 2 positions.
12. a
    The L-shape alternates left/right; the circle/triangle/square moves 1 place up (bottom one shaded); the number of dots decreases by 1, each one turning into a cross before being replaced with a dash.

Section 4
E.g. d
   The only figure not made up of a quadrilateral and a triangle touching by the sides.
P1. c
   The only figure in which the corner square is not shaded.
P2. d
   The only figure with a shaded arrowhead.
1. c
   All other arrows are anticlockwise.
2. c
   All other shapes, moving down, are shaded dark, white and vertically striped.
3. d
   Only figure with greater number of sides on the left than the right.
4. a
   Only figure with small shape on the left.
5. e
   Other figures have, moving clockwise, circle, triangle, square.

6. b
   Other figures have a dot in exactly half of the sections.
7. b
   Other figures have the smallest shape in the middle.
8. e
   Other figures have a dark dot on a corner.
9. c
   Only figure with arrow pointing to intersection rather than away from it.
10. a
    Only figure with an even number of dots.
11. a
    Only figure where the 2 small shapes are different shapes.
12. d
    Other figures have the same number of dots as curves.

Section 5
E.g. 1.d
   The top letter is for the shape, the bottom letter for the dividing line. N stands for circle, V for square; R for vertical dividing line, P for horizontal.
E.g. 2.b
   The top letter is for the shapes on either side of the line, the bottom for the single or double line. O stands for circles, P for squares, S for triangles; T stands for single line, M for double.
P1. b
   White triangle = R; figure in top left = Z: RZ
P2. a
   Circles = N; 3 concentric shapes = M: NM
P3. e
   Dark circle in the centre = B; dark circle at top = U: BU
1. e
   Horizontal stripe = M; central square = R: MR
2. e
   1 shaded dot each end but no shaded dot in middle of line = H; lozenge and triangle = T: HT
3. b
   6 petals = S; cross in centre = M: SM
4. a
   Irregular pentagon = D; 3 short lines = W: DW
5. c
   Horizontal stripe = A; dashed out-line = C: AC
6. e
   Double arrowhead = L; double squares = I: LI
7. b
   Top and bottom shaded = F; circles = V: FV
8. a
   Anticlockwise arrow = Z; fine arrowhead and perpendicular line at other end of the arrow = Y: ZY
9. d
   Diagonal stripe bottom left to top right = O; dot top left = K: OK
10. c
    Dark scallops = D; equilateral triangle = B: DB
11. a
    Dark curve = G; dot at top centre = V: GV
12. a
    Horizontal line = J; positioned at bottom = W: JW

Notes

Notes

Notes

Pupil's Name		Date of Test

School Name	

PUPIL NUMBER

[0]	[0]	[0]	[0]	[0]	[0]
[1]	[1]	[1]	[1]	[1]	[1]
[2]	[2]	[2]	[2]	[2]	[2]
[3]	[3]	[3]	[3]	[3]	[3]
[4]	[4]	[4]	[4]	[4]	[4]
[5]	[5]	[5]	[5]	[5]	[5]
[6]	[6]	[6]	[6]	[6]	[6]
[7]	[7]	[7]	[7]	[7]	[7]
[8]	[8]	[8]	[8]	[8]	[8]
[9]	[9]	[9]	[9]	[9]	[9]

SCHOOL NUMBER

[0]	[0]	[0]	[0]	[0]	[0]	[0]
[1]	[1]	[1]	[1]	[1]	[1]	[1]
[2]	[2]	[2]	[2]	[2]	[2]	[2]
[3]	[3]	[3]	[3]	[3]	[3]	[3]
[4]	[4]	[4]	[4]	[4]	[4]	[4]
[5]	[5]	[5]	[5]	[5]	[5]	[5]
[6]	[6]	[6]	[6]	[6]	[6]	[6]
[7]	[7]	[7]	[7]	[7]	[7]	[7]
[8]	[8]	[8]	[8]	[8]	[8]	[8]
[9]	[9]	[9]	[9]	[9]	[9]	[9]

DATE OF BIRTH

Day		Month		Year	
[0]	[0]	January		2007	
[1]	[1]	February		2008	
[2]	[2]	March		2009	
[3]	[3]	April		2010	
	[4]	May		2011	
	[5]	June		2012	
	[6]	July		2013	
	[7]	August		2014	
	[8]	September		2015	
	[9]	October		2016	
		November		2017	
		December		2018	

Please mark like this ⊟.

SECTION 1

SECTION 2

PUPIL NUMBER

[0]	[0]	[0]	[0]	[0]	[0]
[1]	[1]	[1]	[1]	[1]	[1]
[2]	[2]	[2]	[2]	[2]	[2]
[3]	[3]	[3]	[3]	[3]	[3]
[4]	[4]	[4]	[4]	[4]	[4]
[5]	[5]	[5]	[5]	[5]	[5]
[6]	[6]	[6]	[6]	[6]	[6]
[7]	[7]	[7]	[7]	[7]	[7]
[8]	[8]	[8]	[8]	[8]	[8]
[9]	[9]	[9]	[9]	[9]	[9]

SECTION 3

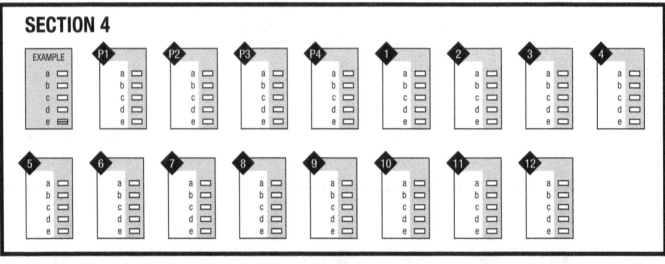

SECTION 4

SECTION 5

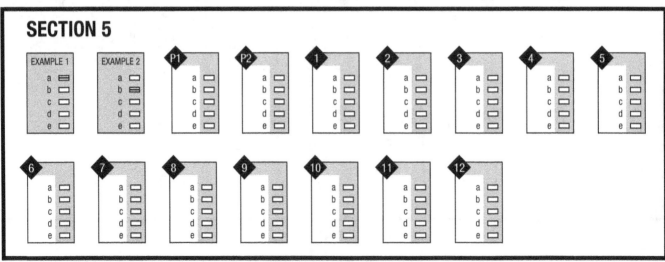

Pupil's Name

School Name

Date of Test

PUPIL NUMBER

[0]	[0]	[0]	[0]	[0]	[0]
[1]	[1]	[1]	[1]	[1]	[1]
[2]	[2]	[2]	[2]	[2]	[2]
[3]	[3]	[3]	[3]	[3]	[3]
[4]	[4]	[4]	[4]	[4]	[4]
[5]	[5]	[5]	[5]	[5]	[5]
[6]	[6]	[6]	[6]	[6]	[6]
[7]	[7]	[7]	[7]	[7]	[7]
[8]	[8]	[8]	[8]	[8]	[8]
[9]	[9]	[9]	[9]	[9]	[9]

SCHOOL NUMBER

[0]	[0]	[0]	[0]	[0]	[0]	[0]
[1]	[1]	[1]	[1]	[1]	[1]	[1]
[2]	[2]	[2]	[2]	[2]	[2]	[2]
[3]	[3]	[3]	[3]	[3]	[3]	[3]
[4]	[4]	[4]	[4]	[4]	[4]	[4]
[5]	[5]	[5]	[5]	[5]	[5]	[5]
[6]	[6]	[6]	[6]	[6]	[6]	[6]
[7]	[7]	[7]	[7]	[7]	[7]	[7]
[8]	[8]	[8]	[8]	[8]	[8]	[8]
[9]	[9]	[9]	[9]	[9]	[9]	[9]

DATE OF BIRTH

Day		Month		Year	
[0]	[0]	January	▭	2007	▭
[1]	[1]	February	▭	2008	▭
[2]	[2]	March	▭	2009	▭
[3]	[3]	April	▭	2010	▭
	[4]	May	▭	2011	▭
	[5]	June	▭	2012	▭
	[6]	July	▭	2013	▭
	[7]	August	▭	2014	▭
	[8]	September	▭	2015	▭
	[9]	October	▭	2016	▭
		November	▭	2017	▭
		December	▭	2018	▭

Please mark like this ⊢⊣.

SECTION 1

SECTION 2

    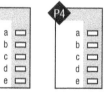

PUPIL NUMBER

[0] [0] [0] [0] [0] [0]
[1] [1] [1] [1] [1] [1]
[2] [2] [2] [2] [2] [2]
[3] [3] [3] [3] [3] [3]
[4] [4] [4] [4] [4] [4]
[5] [5] [5] [5] [5] [5]
[6] [6] [6] [6] [6] [6]
[7] [7] [7] [7] [7] [7]
[8] [8] [8] [8] [8] [8]
[9] [9] [9] [9] [9] [9]

SECTION 3

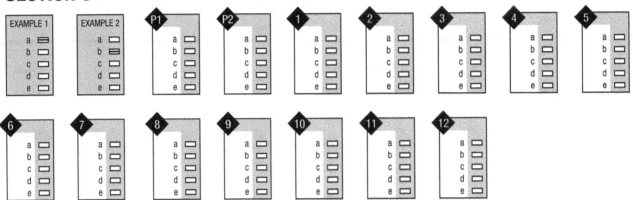

SECTION 4

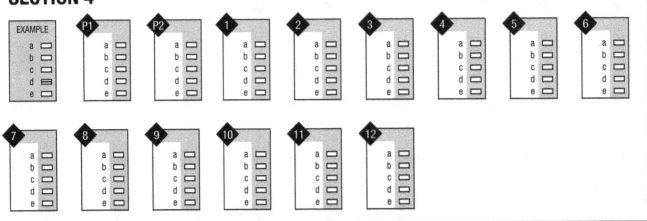

SECTION 5

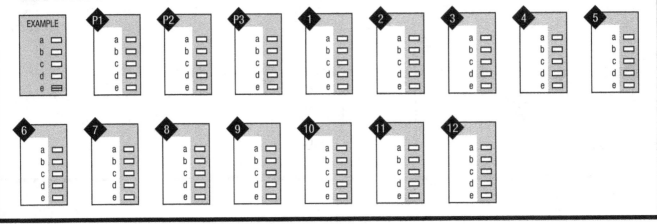

Pupil's Name		Date of Test

School Name	

PUPIL NUMBER

[0]	[0]	[0]	[0]	[0]	[0]
[1]	[1]	[1]	[1]	[1]	[1]
[2]	[2]	[2]	[2]	[2]	[2]
[3]	[3]	[3]	[3]	[3]	[3]
[4]	[4]	[4]	[4]	[4]	[4]
[5]	[5]	[5]	[5]	[5]	[5]
[6]	[6]	[6]	[6]	[6]	[6]
[7]	[7]	[7]	[7]	[7]	[7]
[8]	[8]	[8]	[8]	[8]	[8]
[9]	[9]	[9]	[9]	[9]	[9]

SCHOOL NUMBER

[0]	[0]	[0]	[0]	[0]	[0]	[0]
[1]	[1]	[1]	[1]	[1]	[1]	[1]
[2]	[2]	[2]	[2]	[2]	[2]	[2]
[3]	[3]	[3]	[3]	[3]	[3]	[3]
[4]	[4]	[4]	[4]	[4]	[4]	[4]
[5]	[5]	[5]	[5]	[5]	[5]	[5]
[6]	[6]	[6]	[6]	[6]	[6]	[6]
[7]	[7]	[7]	[7]	[7]	[7]	[7]
[8]	[8]	[8]	[8]	[8]	[8]	[8]
[9]	[9]	[9]	[9]	[9]	[9]	[9]

DATE OF BIRTH

Day		Month		Year	
[0]	[0]	January		2007	
[1]	[1]	February		2008	
[2]	[2]	March		2009	
[3]	[3]	April		2010	
	[4]	May		2011	
	[5]	June		2012	
	[6]	July		2013	
	[7]	August		2014	
	[8]	September		2015	
	[9]	October		2016	
		November		2017	
		December		2018	

Please mark like this ⊟.

SECTION 1

SECTION 2

         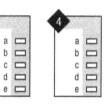

PUPIL NUMBER

[0]	[0]	[0]	[0]	[0]	[0]
[1]	[1]	[1]	[1]	[1]	[1]
[2]	[2]	[2]	[2]	[2]	[2]
[3]	[3]	[3]	[3]	[3]	[3]
[4]	[4]	[4]	[4]	[4]	[4]
[5]	[5]	[5]	[5]	[5]	[5]
[6]	[6]	[6]	[6]	[6]	[6]
[7]	[7]	[7]	[7]	[7]	[7]
[8]	[8]	[8]	[8]	[8]	[8]
[9]	[9]	[9]	[9]	[9]	[9]

SECTION 3

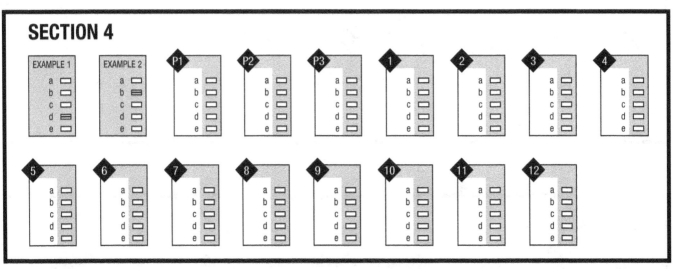

SECTION 4

SECTION 5

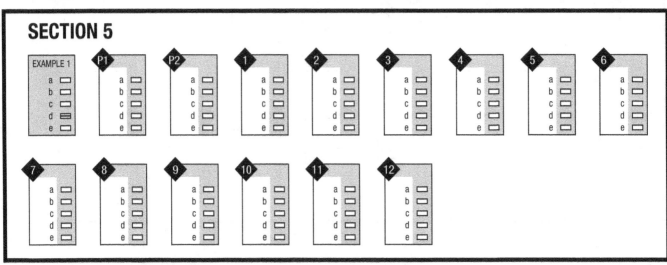

Pupil's Name

School Name

Date of Test

DATE OF BIRTH

Day		Month		Year	
[0]	[0]	January	☐	2007	☐
[1]	[1]	February	☐	2008	☐
[2]	[2]	March	☐	2009	☐
[3]	[3]	April	☐	2010	☐
	[4]	May	☐	2011	☐
	[5]	June	☐	2012	☐
	[6]	July	☐	2013	☐
	[7]	August	☐	2014	☐
	[8]	September	☐	2015	☐
	[9]	October	☐	2016	☐
		November	☐	2017	☐
		December	☐	2018	☐

PUPIL NUMBER

[0]	[0]	[0]	[0]	[0]	[0]
[1]	[1]	[1]	[1]	[1]	[1]
[2]	[2]	[2]	[2]	[2]	[2]
[3]	[3]	[3]	[3]	[3]	[3]
[4]	[4]	[4]	[4]	[4]	[4]
[5]	[5]	[5]	[5]	[5]	[5]
[6]	[6]	[6]	[6]	[6]	[6]
[7]	[7]	[7]	[7]	[7]	[7]
[8]	[8]	[8]	[8]	[8]	[8]
[9]	[9]	[9]	[9]	[9]	[9]

SCHOOL NUMBER

[0]	[0]	[0]	[0]	[0]	[0]	[0]
[1]	[1]	[1]	[1]	[1]	[1]	[1]
[2]	[2]	[2]	[2]	[2]	[2]	[2]
[3]	[3]	[3]	[3]	[3]	[3]	[3]
[4]	[4]	[4]	[4]	[4]	[4]	[4]
[5]	[5]	[5]	[5]	[5]	[5]	[5]
[6]	[6]	[6]	[6]	[6]	[6]	[6]
[7]	[7]	[7]	[7]	[7]	[7]	[7]
[8]	[8]	[8]	[8]	[8]	[8]	[8]
[9]	[9]	[9]	[9]	[9]	[9]	[9]

Please mark like this ⊢.

SECTION 1

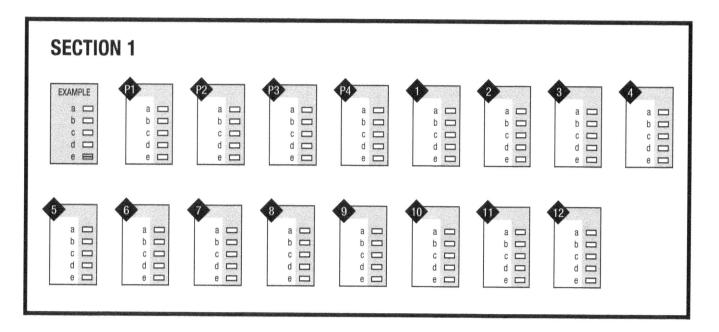

SECTION 2

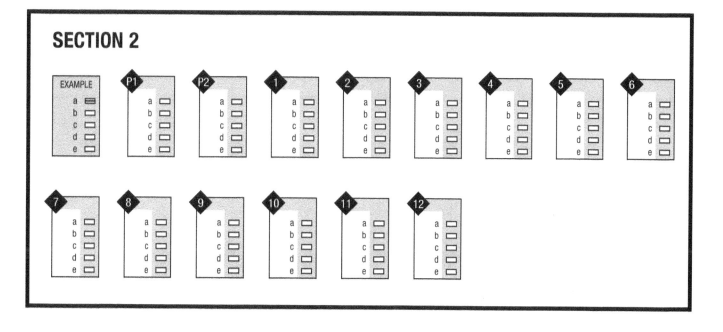

PUPIL NUMBER

[0]	[0]	[0]	[0]	[0]	[0]
[1]	[1]	[1]	[1]	[1]	[1]
[2]	[2]	[2]	[2]	[2]	[2]
[3]	[3]	[3]	[3]	[3]	[3]
[4]	[4]	[4]	[4]	[4]	[4]
[5]	[5]	[5]	[5]	[5]	[5]
[6]	[6]	[6]	[6]	[6]	[6]
[7]	[7]	[7]	[7]	[7]	[7]
[8]	[8]	[8]	[8]	[8]	[8]
[9]	[9]	[9]	[9]	[9]	[9]

SECTION 3

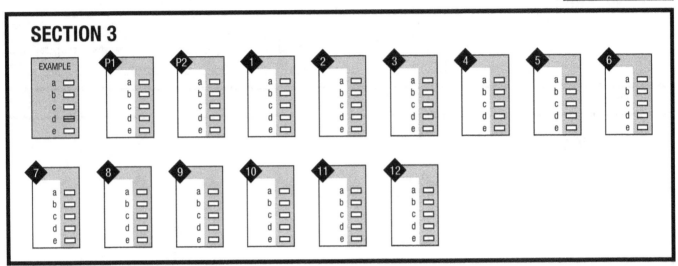

SECTION 4

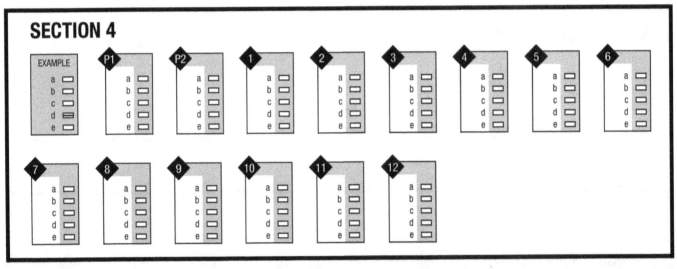

SECTION 5

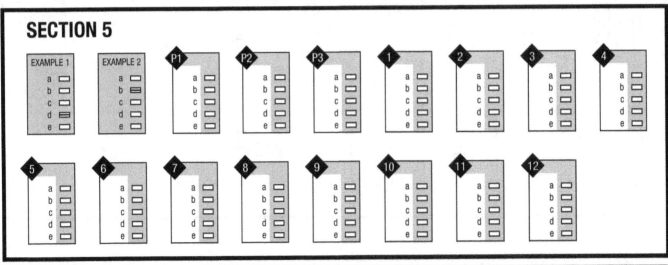

© HarperCollins*Publishers*